March 9th. 1943

To
Marjorie

on her birthday

from Daddy.

GHOSTS OF LONDON

CHELSEA PENSIONERS IN CHAPEL

GHOSTS

OF

LONDON

~~~~~~~~~~~~~~~~~~~~

BY

H. V. MORTON

Illustrated
From Photographs
and with Drawings by
JAMES MACDONALD

~~~~~~~~~~~~~~~~~~~~

DODD, MEAD AND COMPANY
NEW YORK 1940

GHOSTS OF LONDON

Published February 1940
Second Printing March 1940

PRINTED IN THE UNITED STATES OF AMERICA
BY THE VAIL-BALLOU PRESS, INC., BINGHAMTON, N. Y.

CONTENTS

CONTENTS

ILLUSTRATIONS

GHOSTS OF LONDON

CHAPTER

1

THE GHOSTS OF LONDON

I turned on the wireless one still autumn morning, the 3rd
of September, 1939, and heard that we were at war with
Germany. In a twinkling the world had changed, and once
again the word "finish" had been written to a chapter of
one's life. I had the feeling, which strengthened with the days
that followed, that the past twenty odd years had been a
dream and that we were back again where we had left off in

November, 1918. But we of the last War are a little shorter
of breath; we are not quite so young in the evening as in the
morning, and perhaps some of us would not fit as neatly as
we once did into that uncompromising gauge of contour,
the belt designed by General Samuel Browne.

Among the many things which I put away for the dura-
tion of the War were the proofs of this book. But publishers
are an obdurate race, and I was soon asked to return them
for publication. I pointed out that I had other things to do,
and that the pre-war title was, to say the least of it, tactless
now that half London had been recruited and trained with
the object of preventing the other half from becoming
ghosts. Still I was asked to return them, and I began to think
that perhaps it might be interesting to launch this little book,
because its theme is something we should keep in mind: the
continuity of London's existence.

In times of peace it is permissible for all but a few antiquaries to forget the past and to forge ahead cheerfully into
the future; but in wartime a nation, calling up its spiritual
reserves, draws unconsciously upon the strength of its past,
and owes to its ancestors more than it knows, or than may
be set down in words. So if these sketches of a past that still
influences the present have any interest, it is because they
remind us of certain permanent values, and they promise
that London, so old in experience, will one day pick up the
threads of her existence and go onward in history.

Unlike the War of 1914, this War of 1939 has already interrupted the normal life of London as nothing has done since the Norman Conquest, except, maybe, the Great Plague and the Fire in the time of Charles II. Such calamities are not, however, a true parallel with present events, because Stuart London was only an over-grown country town that was facing the common scourge of all large towns since the Middle Ages. Modern London faces an unpredictable peril: the peril of war in the air waged for the first time on a large scale upon one of the world's great capitals. The recent experiences of Madrid, Barcelona, and Warsaw, and our acquaintance with Zeppelin and Gotha raids during the last War, are some indication of the perils which may threaten us. What Londoners are witnessing to-day is something unparalleled in the city's history. A capital with a population of eight million people, the greatest of the world's capitals, has suddenly begun to decentralize itself because it is threatened from the air. In so doing, London has attempted to undo the work of centuries. All roads have led to her since the great Elizabethan trade expansion; but for a time all roads now lead away from her. I think it is probably true to say that those who live through any remarkable experience often accept it as a matter of course. It is only afterwards, from a sufficient vantage-point in time, that its full significance is seen; and I am sure that few people in London at the moment are aware that they are the eye-witnesses of the most remarkable event in the city's history since the end of the Roman occupation.

Like thousands of my fellow countrymen, I decided the other day to make a new Will, and in wartime one makes a new Will without any of the havering or self-pity which attends this act in normal times. An age in which every householder has a gas-mask, and in which every other garden has its optimistic bomb-proof shelter, is obviously not one in which the making of a Will is attended by any drama. When I rang up my solicitor to ask him to be kind enough to send me my Will, a harassed voice at the other end of the wire replied that all documents had been removed to a place of safety in the country, and it would be impossible to obtain the Will for several days. By these strange sidelights is the Londoner made aware that such apparently changeless things as the routine of a solicitor's office, which is assumed to be as immutable as the tides, have suffered a change; by such sidelights is he aware that London is not quite the same as it was. If you could see my solicitor's office, which was last dusted in the eighteenth century, you would understand why the information that all the tin boxes had been sent to some improbable rural destination brought home to me the unparalleled character of the times in which we live. The benign founder of the firm would have had no difficulty in believing that Britain would one day fight a war of principle, but nothing would have convinced him that any war would necessitate the firm's migration to Little Mudworthy; neither would he have believed that it could function from any place but that crusted and panelled portion of London known to the Post Office as W.C.2.

However, my Will, in company with more valuable objects, such as the Elgin Marbles, the Tintorettos, the Gainsboroughs, Domesday Book, and Magna Charta, had been spirited from its usual resting-place, and such knowledge, multiplied a thousand-fold, brings with it the realization that Bismarck's famous dictum has been brought to nothing; for the sacker of London would now get precious little for his pains. It remains to be seen whether London will accept decentralization, or whether, like women of the evacuated areas, she prefers to die in her own alley rather than face the rigours of a rural life. All one can say for the moment is that London is learning the infinite possibilities of necessity.

It would have surprised many of my readers in the Dominions and Colonies, and in the United States, could they have travelled up to London with me the other day. It was a brilliant September morning, and high gold clouds moved against a blue sky. As we approached Waterloo Station, my fellow passengers, each one carrying a small box containing a gas-mask, crowded to the windows to admire the balloon barrage, the most beautiful sight London has seen for many a year. When the sun is shining, the air above London is dotted with hundreds of glistening balloons. They fly in picturesque companies at varying heights, and sometimes, when the light falls in a certain way, you can see the cable, slender, it seems, as a spider's web, which anchors them to earth. The balloons are not globular, but shaped like airships. They swing with the wind and hang facing the same way, like yachts in harbour. This gives them a watchful, purposeful air which is in strange contrast to their air of gaiety, almost of gala, which small children recognize at once and hail with pleasure. It is perhaps strange that this death-trap should look more like a carnival than anything London has ever attempted in the way of decoration. Had they been flown for the Coronation, no voice would have been raised in protest.

Arriving in London, the visitor looks round him with some astonishment. He enters a city which exists, as Athens, Rome and Constantinople have done at critical moments of their history, in a state of watchful expectancy. Whereas in ancient times a city manned its walls and accepted within them an additional population from the surrounding country, a modern city sends away refugees instead of accepting them, and mans, not its walls, but its fire stations, its fire alarms and its cellars. As I drove through London in a taxicab, still driven, I am glad to say, by an ironic Cockney, I saw everywhere members of the civilian army of defence. That civilians should defend a city in time of need is no new thing, but it is such a novel sight in modern England that I looked curiously at the large number of my fellow citizens who stood, thinly disguised by shrapnel helmets and armlets, directing the traffic, standing beside sandbagged fire-alarms, and patrolling the streets, ready at the sound of a siren to shepherd the passer-by to a place of safety.

My memories of London during the War of 1914–18 are associated mainly with hot baths, food and theatres. On those rare occasions when I moved carelessly in the subaltern's London of that time, I seem to recollect a warm and cheering background of life against which could be read the slogan: "Business as Usual." It is a slogan that cannot be used in the London of this war. Business is still in progress, but it is not "as usual." A placard, as prominent in this war as the one I have mentioned was prominent in the last, bears the words: "Air Raid Shelter"; and such notices are pasted everywhere on shop windows and on buildings, sometimes with an arrow pointing downwards in the direction of a basement.

What gives London its strange new appearance are the emptiness of its streets, particularly west of Charing Cross, and the incredible deformity of sandbagged buildings and windows criss-crossed with strips of gummed paper. As he walks the streets of London to-day, the veteran of the last war might well reflect that something of the appearance of the Ypres Salient has come to the capital; and it is still with incredulity that one enters a bank between a six-foot rampart, or sits in a favourite restaurant whose rooms are darkened by the sandbags piled outside. And another thing that has impressed me about this new London is that its sound has altered: the deep, uniform throb of the traffic has dropped in tone, and through the diminished sound can always be heard the explosions of police and military motor-bicycles. This imparts to London a throbbing note of urgency. As I listened to the altered sound of London, I reflected that in the far-off days "before the war"—otherwise a fortnight ago—the sound of a motor-bicycle was rarely, if ever, heard in the Strand, and never, I am sure, in Piccadilly.

Of all the war news from the London front, nothing has impressed me more than the information that one of the dairy companies is to sell half its ponies. So many people are away from London, it is said, that many ponies have no work to do, and fodder is to be rationed. To anyone fond, as I am, of wandering about London before breakfast, watching the giant stretch his arms and yawn his way into a new day, the absence of those rotund little creatures, harnessed to miniature lorries on pneumatic tires, each creature bearing a name like "Doris" or "Mabel" on a head-collar, is a loss I do not like to contemplate. The morning milkman and his pony were, I always thought, among those attractive features of London life so familiar to us that we hardly noticed them.

I had occasion to go to the War Office one morning, and there I saw something which amused me because it was so typical of London. The same crowd of women that I have often seen gathered at the gates of St. Margaret's, waiting for the bride, were standing round the steps of the War Office, each woman grasping a gas-mask, waiting for generals. You might have expected them, in deference to the times, to be wearing a worn or an anxious expression, for nearly every wall was plastered with air-raid advice, but the expression they wore was the same placid and appreciative one which they used to wear at St. Margaret's. I felt certain that could I have waited until a general emerged, I should have heard them give, from force of habit, that long-drawn sigh of matrimonial approval: "Oooh, ain't he lovely!" No matter what happens to us in this war, there will always be Londoners to stand and watch it, and I think Macaulay showed little knowledge of London when he gave to a New Zealander the privilege of gazing at the ruins of St. Paul's. That is a spectacle which no true Londoner would ever be denied.

One of the strangest things about this war is the return to life and popularity of the London cellar. For many years those of us who inhabit Georgian or Victorian houses in London have literally looked down upon our cellars as on something shameful. Those of us who had the curiosity to explore them, discovered with surprise the enormous amount of space reserved by our ancestors for wine and coal. In an age of electricity and cocktails, there seemed to be no possible use for a cellar except perhaps to a photographer or a coiner; and the house agents, aware of the positive hatred which cellars roused, especially in the minds of women, began to attract purchasers with promises of "non-basement residences." But all that is now changed, and a good big cellar is the finest asset a house can have. Reinforced with timber and concrete, the cool catacombs in which grandfather kept his port and madeira have become our refuge in a world at war.

It is not now unusual in London to be taken down into a cellar and to be shown round it by the owner. This happened to me when I visited my tailor. Hearing some determined noises beneath his shop, I asked what was happening, and was told that the cellars were being transformed into an official air-raid shelter. He asked me politely if I would care to step down and have a look at it, and so I followed the pool of his electric torch down a flight of stone steps into a crypt. We were in a vaulted Georgian cellar, or it might have been even slightly earlier, and the whole place had been framed with enormous baulks of timber. With a bewildered pride, the tailor told me that it was estimated by the municipal authorities that if the whole house collapsed, the reinforced cellar could hold the weight of it. There was a sinister little concrete circle through which a human being could just about crawl on his hands and knees, and this led under the street. I was told that it was the emergency exit. There is something entirely preposterous and macabre about such preparations, but the most surprising thing about them is that we accept them now as casually as we accept our gas-masks.

The gas-mask is a tedious but compulsory companion, which may be carried in a number of ways: in the hard, square box in which it was issued; in a haversack; in a camera-case; or in a tin. As everybody is supposed to carry this object with him wherever he goes, and as most people do so, the effect in the streets of London is of a population that has become addicted to sandwiches or amateur photography. In a pathetic attempt to live the old life, a number of shops have devised smart little cases of shining leather and cloth in many brilliant colours, but such things are obviously out of tune with the times: one cannot feel any pride in the ownership of a gas-mask.

When these days are over we shall, no doubt, look back with grim amusement upon the inconveniences, the absurdities, the humiliations of this war. We shall remember the horrid awakenings to the sound of a radio crooner just before 8 a.m.; and there is no time in the twenty-four hours when syncopation is less soothing to the spirit. Soon the voice of a yearning vocalist, telling us that he doesn't mind the coldest December wind and snow because he is warm with love, is faded out to make way for an official voice telling us how to make the basement blast-proof. What an awakening to a new day! Then, at night, what householder will ever forget the dreary perambulation round his house to see that no chink in blind or curtain admits a beam of light into the darkness; what householder will forget those moments in the night when, wrestling with his soul, he wonders if the cook will give notice if he dares to tell her that, as usual, the kitchen is signalling to the enemy.

To those who have known London for years, the most remarkable of all our precautions is the nightly "black-out."

As dusk approaches, shops close and the assistants take part in that nightly event of war-time London: getting home before the "black-out." Gradually the light dies, until the whole city is dark. It is so black that a man travelling in an omnibus cannot tell whether he has offered the conductor a penny or half a crown until he has felt the milled edge with his nail. It is so black that a man has to tap his way across streets that he has known all his life. Who moves in the blackness I do not know, but it is made sinister by the presence of invisible people close to one, sometimes touching one as they feel and tap their way about. A jet-black Piccadilly is something that was never contemplated by any previous generation, and one has the eerie impression of being lost in some city of the dead. It is a new experience to perceive the Swan and Edgar Corner by sense of touch! By the time these words appear in print, a little more light may have been decreed, but in these first weeks of war London, on a moonless night, knows the state of the wandering stars of *Revelation*, "to whom is reserved the blackness of darkness for ever."

When the pale autumn dawn comes over London, and still no bomb has fallen, the Londoner rises and, with a feeling of anti-climax, goes down to the inconvenienced city. "This is a very strange war," he says. "You wait," says his friend. "It hasn't started yet."

These outward changes in London's appearance should indicate, of course, a corresponding change in the Londoner's attitude to life. But I have never seen London calmer, or the Londoner more deliberate in his ways. He is determined to carry on as if nothing had happened, even though his office and the streets he knows so well have been invaded by an atmosphere of makeshift and picnic. It is amusing to read in unfriendly countries accounts of London's fear and panic; for those are the two emotions you will not encounter in our streets. I had always imagined that there must be something obviously heroic about a city on the defensive, and so, indeed, there is beneath the surface. But outwardly there is not. London has prepared to meet war in the air in much the same way that she might organize herself to fight a plague of rats.

In prefacing the following sketches of London history with these few impressions of war-time London, I do so with the knowledge that the times in which we are living will take their place among the sterner annals of the city. Apart from the air-raids of the last war, and the occasion, in 1667, when De Ruyter's guns were heard on the Thames, London has known nothing of war. The London that Boadicea sacked and burned to the ground is so far off that we can hardly claim kinship with her. Therefore, equally with Paris and Berlin, she stands on the threshold of a new experience; and one which may demand from her courage and fortitude.

But let us turn from the London of to-day and go back into the London in which I gathered this mosaic of ancient custom. Here we see an old and famous city keeping appointment with her past, remembering things that she thought worth remembering, and treasuring certain events from century to century, embodying them in current ceremony and custom. Though many of these treasured memories may lapse during the days ahead, the time will come when they will return to take their place in the rich pageantry of London life. Wars come to an end, but London goes on.

CHAPTER

2

"CHARLIE'S DAY"

When I was a boy, I remember how children in Warwick-
shire looked forward to Oak Apple Day, the 29th of May.
Early in the morning we would go out into the woods and
pick sprigs of oak, taking care to pick those which had oak-
apples attached to them. Wearing them in our caps or pinned
to our jackets, we would then gather stinging nettles and,
protecting our hands by wrapping paper or handkerchiefs

round the stalks, we would roam about in search of boys who were not wearing oak leaves.

The encounters were violent and determined. If a boy could not produce a sprig of oak, it would be the signal for us to sting him across his bare knees or his hands with the nettles. I seem to remember, but I could not swear to this, that, as we administered this barbaric punishment, we shouted the word "Traitor." It often happened that some of the largest and most dangerous boys were those who had failed to wear oak leaves, and many a time we were stung by our own nettles.

Not one of us, I believe, had the slightest idea why he did this; it probably never occurred to us to inquire. I am sure that no grown-up persons who, as all children know, live in a sentimental network of sometimes rich and profitable anniversaries, ever reminded us that the 29th of May was approaching, and the process whereby large numbers of boys became annually aware of Oak Apple Day seems to me, at this distance of time, mysterious and unaccountable.

But is it any more mysterious than the approach of November 5th, which regularly every year warns London children to go forth into the October streets with a Guy Fawkes in a perambulator? Or is it more mysterious than the recollection that grotto time has come, which is the last surviving memory in England of the great Catholic pilgrimages to St. James of Compostella? Such childish observances of once national events are memories moving dimly in the minds of the youngest members of the race, and it is surely curious that children should often be the custodians of ceremonies which have long since ceased to be celebrated by their elders.

Oak Apple Day, or May 29th, was the birthday of Charles II, and it was upon that day, his thirtieth birthday, that the king made his triumphal entry into London after twelve years of exile. This country has rarely shown less restraint in its joy, for when the king returned to "enjoy his own again," the gloomy clouds of the Puritan dictatorship seemed finally dispelled. The splendid story of the wanderings of Charles II after the Battle of Worcester, a story every bit as romantic as the wanderings of another Charlie, were of course recent memories, and among the royal adventures none was more celebrated than the story of the Boscobel Oak.

I do not think you will find anywhere in English history a more romantic story than the six weeks' wanderings of Charles II after Cromwell had "beaten him from hedge to hedge" in Worcester. With a reward of £1,000 on his head, and the land alive with Parliament troops, that young man of twenty-one, disguised in a shabby doublet and a threadbare coat of green, with a greasy Puritan hat on his shorn locks and his face darkened with walnut juice, passed through the hands of over forty people, most of them poor and humble, not one of whom betrayed him.

We see him plunging into wet ditches, lying under hedges, climbing fences at the edge of woodlands by the light of the moon, kicking off his heavy country shoes and staggering on with bleeding feet. The candle-light falls on him in humble houses. Joan Penderel heals the blisters on his feet and packs little wads of paper between his bruised toes.

One morning the red-coats look for him in Boscobel. He slips out to Boscobel Wood where, in the heavy branches of a great oak, he lies for twenty-four hours with Colonel Careless, a cavalryman who saw the last man killed at Worcester. The troopers beat the wood in search of the King, and Charles, tired after days and nights in the open, falls asleep with his head on his companion's lap.

Then, disguised as a farmer's son and answering to the name of William Jackson, the King of England sets out, with Mistress Jane Lane riding pillion behind him, holding on to his belt. There is a breath-catching moment in Stratford-on-Avon when a company of Cromwell's horse turns a corner. But Charles rides straight on, and the troops part to let the "country lad" and his mistress pass on their journey.

Once or twice Charles nearly gives himself away. Supping one night with the servants in a hall, a maid tells him to turn the spit. But the King does not know how to do so. The servants gather round laughing to see this strange lad, and Charles extricates himself by saying, "Up in Staffordshire, where I come from, we don't often eat meat." And they believe him. With his hair cropped close and the sombre Puritan hat shading his solemn, dark face, the King stops at many a wayside tavern for a drink.

In one of them the innkeeper takes him into the cellar and says, "You look an honest fellow. Here's a health to the King!" but Charles hesitates to drink his own health, and the innkeeper taunts him for a Roundhead.

There is another delightful scene, when Charles's sallow face under his dark hat brings down on him the taunts of Royalists who, had they only guessed his identity, would have fallen on their knees. On one such occasion Charles is forced to play the Puritan and to rebuke a drunken cavalier with the words: "O dear brother, swear not, I beseech you!"

At last the day comes when, from a little creek at Shoreham, near Brighton, a coal brig, the *Surprise,* lifts her sails and puts to sea. The crew of four men and a boy are deeply interested in the tall, dark young man with the clipped hair who walks the deck and offers to take the wheel.

On May 29th, nine years later, the same tall, dark man rides bareheaded into London while the steeples rock with joy and guns are fired. And so begins the Restoration.

During the nine years which elapsed from the flight of Charles to the Restoration, the hair-breadth escapes of the King were on the lips of all cavaliers, and the Royal Oak became a symbol of loyalty to the Crown. No sooner was Charles restored to his Kingdom than a whole crop of ballads and broadsides, which probably represented the songs and stories that during the Commonwealth had been sung and told behind closed doors, burst fearlessly on the public. Mr. A. M. Broadley, who collected such literature, has reprinted much of it in a book called *The Royal Miracle,* and we can see for ourselves that no incident pleased the public so much as the story of the oak in whose boughs the king lay in safety, while the Roundheads beat the woods for him in vain.

The oak tree became the symbol of English loyalty, and the sign of "The Royal Oak" was soon popular with tavern keepers, who displayed pictures showing the King hiding in the boughs, or peeping down at his pursuers through the greenery. It was not long before the country people of England transferred the gaiety of the older May Day to the anniversary of the Restoration, and in every village in the land houses were decorated with oak boughs and gilded oak-apples, while men went about wearing oak leaves in their caps, and the villagers danced round an oak-wreathed maypole on the green.

Parliament enacted at this time

that in all succeeding ages the 29th of May be celebrated in every church and chapel of England and the Dominions thereof by rendering thanks to God for the King's peaceable restoration to actual possession and exercise of his legal authority over his subjects.

And this day, known to the common people as Oak Apple Day, remained an official day of rejoicing until the year

1859. Among the ghosts of London is an attractive survival of Oak Apple Day. Every 29th of May the Chelsea Pensioners parade before the mounted statue of Charles II in the forecourt of the Royal Hospital, and for this occasion the statue is decorated with boughs of oak. The old soldiers polish up their medals for this parade, which is known to them as "Charlie's Day," and they stand to attention in their scarlet coats as the Governor calls out:

"Three cheers for the King!"

A wavering cheer rises from the veterans, but it is not for King George VI; it is for King Charles II, the founder of the Royal Hospital.

In order that there shall be no mistake about it, the next command is:

"Three cheers for King George!"

Then the old men march past. When the parade is over they receive an extra pint of beer in memory of the hunted young man in the oak leaves, the King who, in spite of the saddest pair of eyes in history, has gone down to posterity as "the merry monarch."

Describing this ceremony in a newspaper some years ago, I asked whether any children in England still gathered oak leaves and nettles on May 29th, as I did when I was a boy; and I had not long to wait for an answer. For the next few days I was busy opening letters from correspondents in all parts of the country who used to observe Oak Apple Day in their youth, or from those who can testify to the fact that the custom is still observed by young people.

I was told that in the West of England children, having gathered their oak-apples, would march to school singing:

It's Oak Apple Day,
The twenty-ninth of May,
If you don't give us a holiday
We'll all run away.

The same rhyme is sung, so I am informed by a Shropshire correspondent, by the children at Forest of Hayes School, who appear annually with oak-apples and nettles. A reader, who lives on the borders of Northamptonshire and War-wickshire, says that when he was at school the same rhyme was sung, and some of the bolder lads did absent themselves on Oak Apple Day, to be rewarded on the morrow with two strokes of the cane. "But it was worth it," he says. He notes that it was a point of honour amongst boys not to pick the oak-apples the night before, but to rise at an unusually early hour on the morning of the 29th and go out to the woods. Here a touch of gallantry entered into the proceedings which I have found in no other account of Oak Apple Day: it is rather reminiscent of the old May Day celebrations. My correspondent says that it was the custom for the boys to present the girls with a sprig of oak, for which "they were usually rewarded with a kiss."

Many writers in Staffordshire, especially in the Burton-on-Trent district, tell me that Oak Apple Day is still religiously observed by the children. One school teacher at Stretton, near Burton-on-Trent, tells me that, though the children wear sprigs of oak, they have ceased to chastise each other with nettles because "they are a little more humane now." But another correspondent from the same district says that oak-apples and nettles are still vigorously employed! Boys who wear oak leaves challenge other boys with the words "Show your oak!" and, if they fail to do so, they sting them with nettles or thistles.

A third correspondent from the Burton-on-Trent district says that the following rhyme is chanted:

Here's my oak and here's my whistle,
(the child whistles)
Show your oak or you'll feel my thistle.

On May 29th [writes a correspondent from Belton, near Loughborough, Leicestershire] children wears sprigs of oak, and if they fail to do so are mercilessly whipped with stinging nettles on bare arms and legs by other children.

The same thing, I am assured, still takes place at Fernhurst in Sussex, in the villages of Essex, Cambridgeshire, Shropshire, Derbyshire, and in nearly all the Midland counties.

At Mapperly, in Derbyshire, which boasts a "Royal Oak" Inn, the name for May 29th is "Oak and Nettle Day." A man of twenty-seven writes to tell me that when he was at school there: "if you were 'loyal' you wore your sprig of oak leaves, but if you were a 'traitor' you were chased by a boy with a bunch of stinging nettles." At Ropley and its district, near Winchester, the children used to wear oak leaves until noon on May 29th, and until noon would sting those who were not wearing oak leaves. The local name for the day was "Chic-Shack Day," but my informant has no idea what this means or how it is derived.

A correspondent who went to school at Exeter in the 'seventies of the last century, tells me that it was the custom for children to cover the oak-apples with gold-leaf and wear them in their buttonholes. In Durham the cathedral choir ascends the central tower on May 29th and sings an anthem of thanksgiving, and in London the Worshipful Company of Grocers hold a Livery Dinner on that date, called the Restoration Feast, and on that occasion the hall and the grand staircase are decorated with boughs of oak.

So it will be seen that the emotion which swept over England when Charles II came back to the throne has not quite died away. In the schoolboy rhymes asking for a holiday and threatening to take one, we may perhaps hear an echo of the time when this day was indeed a national holiday, and in the taunts of "traitor," hurled by small boys at their companions, we can hear quite distinctly the last shouts of the Cavaliers.

CHAPTER

3

HORN-BLOWERS OF THE TEMPLE

On dark evenings in February the Temple wraps itself in shadow, the lamplight spills itself at the corner of old court-yards, and the quiet place returns to the eighteenth century. The noise of Goldsmith's guests and the deliberate tread of Dr. Johnson's well-shod feet would seem more appropriate than the whine of a tramcar from the Embankment.

In the Temple at night you cannot hear much of the Fleet

Street traffic. The high old buildings shut it out. It becomes lost, perhaps, in the little alleys and in the maze of courts. If, for instance, you sit under the plane tree in Fountain Court, the explosive intrusions of the modern world come only from the Embankment and the river, or from the cars of homeward-bound barristers grinding in low gear up Middle Temple Lane.

The real sound of the Temple after dark is the ring of shoe leather on paving-stone and the cry of some young man to a legally-minded student friend:

"Well, I hope you enjoy your dinner."

"Thanks. I hope so, too."

Then follows the crisp ring of footsteps on the flag-stones . . . and a strange and uncanny sound: the low, uneasy moo of an ancient horn.

It is six-thirty. A man in a brass-buttoned frock-coat, wearing a silk hat bound with gold braid, has come out of Middle Temple Hall, and he stands in Fountain Court, holding a long, curved horn to his lips. He is one of the four Warders of the Temple. During the four law terms he appears every night in the ancient courtyards to blow a dinner warning to the students. Though few students can afford to live in the Temple nowadays, the Warder is still calling them, as his predecessors called for untold centuries, to the long tables of Windsor oak which Queen Elizabeth gave to the lawyers long ago.

His first call is made from Fountain Court. He stands

A HORNBLOWER, THE TEMPLE

facing the lawns of Inner Temple Gardens that run down to the Embankment; and there is a legend among the Warders, which is probably true, that in ancient times the first horn was blown across the Thames to call the students from the marshes and the fields on the opposite bank.

He then perambulates the Temple, stopping to blow the horn in New Court, Essex Court, Brick Court, Pump Court, Elm Court and Middle Temple Lane. It is a low, melancholy moo, rather like a diminutive steamboat getting ready to leave port.

When the horn-blower has made his final moo, he returns to Middle Temple Hall, where a pint of old ale is waiting for him, the gift of the legal profession.

Of all the ghosts in this ancient city of ours, the nightly horn-blowing in the Temple is one of the most romantic. We must look far beyond the eighteenth century for the origin of this custom, far beyond the times of the Stuarts, and even of the Tudors: we must look back to the age when the crusading fire swept like a flame over the Christian world.

At that time the Temple was lying among green fields, in the suburbs of London, and was half-way between the City and Charing. It was the English headquarters of that great and powerful crusading order, the Knights Templars. After centuries of gallant work in the Holy Land, the Order became rotted by riches and, earning the jealousy of kings and the disapproval of the Pope, was abolished in 1312.

But the Templars began well enough. A few poor knights went off on the First Crusade, so impoverished that sometimes two were compelled to share one horse. Pledging themselves to fight in poverty, chastity and humility, they settled on the finest site in Jerusalem: the enormous level platform on Mount Moriah, overlooking the Valley of the Kedron, where the Temple of Solomon had once stood. They found that the traditional site of the Israelite Holy of Holies had been turned into a Moslem shrine, the Dome of the Rock, a small mosque in the centre of an immense courtyard designed to be a rival to the great Mosque at Mecca. Hardly altering the building at all, the Templars took it over and turned it into a church, calling themselves the Poor Knights of Christ and of the Temple of Solomon. This soon became shortened into Knights Templars.

The first Temple Church is once again a mosque, but it contains many Christian memorials. You can see the exquisite screen of gilt ironwork placed by the Crusaders round the outcrop of black stone on which, it is believed, once stood the Israelite Altar of Burnt Offerings. In the cave beneath, you can see the niches of the Christian altars.

The Templars grew in numbers and in wealth. The Order became world-wide. The Knights wore white robes to signify the purity of their lives. A large red cross was added later, a sign that they were willing to shed their blood for Christ.

When they travelled, they carried with them a circular

tent, which symbolized the round Tomb of Christ, and in this portable chapel they attended Mass before venturing into battle. This tent was the predecessor of the round churches of the Templars. The little Temple Church in London is the finest surviving example, although England possesses others at Cambridge, Northampton, Little Maplestead, Essex, and a ruined shell of one in Ludlow Castle.

Paris also possessed its Temple Church, but it has now disappeared. It was in this church, once used as a prison, that Louis XVI and Marie Antoinette were confined when the French Revolution broke out. There also the young Dauphin was slowly tortured to death by the barbaric wretch, Simon the Cobbler.

Beside the clear Thames the Knights Templars built their church, their monastery, their cloisters, and on the flat land, which is now Middle Temple lawn, they trained their war horses for the Crusades.

The knights dined silently in hall, and they were summoned by a horn-blower from their devotions and their exercises. When the Order collapsed in disgrace and ruin, its lands passed into other hands. But men continued to dine in hall and still the horn-blower continued to call them to their food. And he will call them this very night.

There is no other place in the world where a man who, by a slight effort of the imagination, might be the ghost of a Crusader, walks out at night to blow a note upon a horn.

 29

CHAPTER
4

A PINCH OF SNUFF

At the top of the Haymarket there is a bow-fronted shop in whose Georgian windows stand ancient tobacco jars and snuff canisters. This shop still sells seventeen different kinds of snuff, including a blend made popular over a century ago by Beau Brummell.

If you buy a tin of snuff in this shop, as I often do, you will discover that the marriage of the Duke and Duchess of

Kent has given an air of improbable vitality to the old-fashioned label on the tin, which announces in antique type that the firm are purveyors of tobacco and foreign snuff to "the Kings of Hanover, the Dukes of Sussex, Cambridge, and the Duchess of Kent." This duchess was, of course, the mother of Queen Victoria.

All those distinguished patrons have vanished from Debrett, but the snuff which they enjoyed so long ago still goes out clothed in an advertisement that is, appropriately enough, an epitaph on a once general social custom. It may amuse those who enjoy odd facts to know that among the old ledgers in this shop is one containing a list of the favourite snuffs used by George IV. One of them, no longer obtainable, was called "Marina."

Snuff-taking, although a ghost of its former self, is more popular than some of us may imagine. The biggest snuff-grinding mill is in Ireland and there are others in the North of England. Compositors, clergymen, policemen, the curators of art galleries, night-watchmen, and others who are not allowed to smoke tobacco when on duty, still enjoy a pinch of snuff. Lawyers, who with their passionate adherence to precedent, carried the habit into the nineteenth century, seem strangely enough to have abandoned it.

The greatest snuff-takers I have known have been newspaper compositors. I remember a compositor years ago who was in the habit of celebrating the foundrywards departure of the home page with Gargantuan draughts of snuff. As soon as the page had left the case-room, he brought a large tin from his pocket and, extending his bare arm, laid a thick trail of powder from the elbow to the wrist. He would then lower his head and pass his great nose in rapid motion along the brown powder. Nothing would be left but a few grains lying among the hairs and the printer's ink. There was something monstrous about the act: it was rather like watching a man drink tumblers of neat brandy. Oddly enough, I never remember to have seen him sneeze, and he had the reputation of never having suffered from a cold.

Snuff was popular in Scotland and on the Continent long before it became fashionable in England. Its use in England is confined to a definite period—from Queen Anne to George IV.

The story of snuff in this country is bound up with Sir George Rooke's expedition to Vigo in 1702. When the English Fleet landed near Cadiz, an enormous plunder was seized, which included cargoes of snuff in galleons that had just returned from Havana.

This loot—said to have been fifty tons in weight—was sold by the sailors in English ports. Wagon loads of snuff are said to have been sold in Portsmouth, Plymouth and Chatham for 3*d*. and 4*d*. a pound. All England began snuffing. At first, the habit was condemned and laughed at by many writers and dramatists, but it could not be killed, even by ridicule. It was taken up everywhere.

All the best remarks of the eighteenth century were accompanied by a pinch of snuff. Steele mentions in the *Spectator* "the rules for offering snuff to a stranger, a friend or a mistress, according to the degrees of familiarity or distance." And these included the Pinch Scornful, the Pinch Surly, the Pinch Politick, the Pinch Careless, and so on.

Women took to the snuff habit as readily as modern women have accepted the cigarette. Naturally they were criticized, but it soon became as usual to offer a snuff-box to a woman as it is to offer a cigarette case to-day. Undoubtedly the most notable female snuff-taker was Mrs. Margaret Thompson, of Boyle Street, Burlington Gardens, who, when she died on April 2, 1776, left a will directing that she was to be buried in snuff!

I, Margaret Thompson [ran this extraordinary document], being of sound mind, etc., desire that when my soul is departed from this wicked world, my body and effects may be disposed of in the manner following:

I desire that all my handkerchiefs that I may have unwashed at the time of my decease, after they have been got together by my old and trusted servant, Sarah Stuart, be put by her, and by her alone, at the bottom of my coffin, which I desire may be made large enough for that purpose, together with a quantity of the best Scotch snuff (in which she knoweth I always had the greatest delight) as will cover my deceased body; and this I desire more especially as it is usual to put flowers into the coffins of departed friends, and nothing can be so precious and fragrant to me as that precious powder.

She commanded that the six greatest snuff-takers in the parish of St. James, Westminster, should be her bearers, and that each one, instead of black, was to wear a snuff-coloured beaver hat. Six maidens were to bear her pall,

each to bear a proper hood and to carry a box filled with the best Scotch snuff to take for their refreshment as they go along. I also desire my old and faithful servant, Sarah Stuart, to walk before the corpse, to distribute every 20 yards a large handful of Scotch snuff to the ground and upon the crowd . . .

Such can be a woman's devotion.

The modern snuff connoisseur goes to the old shop in Haymarket to smell the delicate aroma which enchanted the eighteenth century. This shop supplied snuff to Napoleon when he was at St. Helena. It also composed a snuff for one of the Popes many years ago.

"Up to the year 1820," I was told, "the cigars and tobacco sold were negligible compared with the quantities of snuff. Modern snuff, however, gives no idea of the power and potency of ancient snuff. Our books contain a number of strange old recipes. For instance, grated prunes, port-wine lees, stale old ale and cheese figure in several eighteenth-century recipes for snuff.

"The first snuff gained its fragrance, not from the addition of scents and essences, but from the careful blending of various pulverized tobaccos. Scented snuff became popular later in the eighteenth century.

-C 34 }-

"The most expensive snuff supplied by us a hundred and fifty years ago was called Spanish Bran. It was three pounds a pound. We used to sell with it a little bottle of Vinagrillo, a rose-scented vinegar from Spain. This liquid was used to moisten the snuff. Another curious snuff was Spanish Sabillia, a fine, brick-red powder, which, it was believed, had useful medicinal qualities. It was supposed to harden the gums and was very popular as a tooth paste. There was a steady demand for it until 1890, when it died out.

"It is curious to note from our ledgers how the cigar and the cigarette have crept into favour and how snuff went out. Our earliest mention of a cigarette is in 1852. Very few were sold until 1866, when Russian cigarettes were popular. From that date the sale of snuff fell away and tobacco went up. One of the things which helped to kill the snuff habit was the fashion for white handkerchiefs."

CHAPTER

5

THE HERB SHOP

Excellent herbs had our fathers of old—
Excellent herbs to ease their pain—
Alexanders and Marigold,
Eyebright, Orris, and Elecampane.
Basil, Rocket, Valerian, Rue
(Almost singing themselves they run),
Vervain, Dittany, Call-me-to-you—
Cowslip, Melilot, Rose of the Sun.

THE HERB SHOP

Anything green that grew out of the mould
Was an excellent herb to our fathers of old.

I would like to have taken Mr. Kipling to a shop in Farringdon Street, not far from Ludgate Circus, which still sells "the excellent herbs" of our fathers of old.

Although a hundred and twenty years have passed since first this shop opened its doors, and although fame and success have come to it (for Potter & Clarke are among the largest and best-known manufacturing chemists in Great Britain), they have never forsaken the ancient remedies.

In the old days bunches of dried herbs used to hang from the roof. Nowadays they are either made up in neat packets or sold by weight from boxes whose labels bear such lovely names as "Cherrylaurel," "Bittersweet," "Archangel," "Hedge-Hyssop," "Lady's Slipper" and "Mouse-ear."

I regard this shop as a real ghost of old London, because I do not know another herbalist who has been prescribing for well over a century from the Elizabethan pharmacopeia. I have been told that herbal remedies are becoming fashionable again; but in this shop they have never been out of fashion.

There is still an enormous amount of traditional medical lore among people who remember their grandparents' remedies and, while much of it may be nonsense, a proportion of it has, time and again, succeeded where the modern doctor and the druggist have failed. There is no question about this. The lore of our ancestors was not all moonshine. That one of the best-known chemists in the country has gone on quietly selling ancient remedies for a century and a quarter speaks itself for the efficacy of herbs.

When I was there the other day, a man came in and asked for "Half a pound of Slippery Elm."

"So you know the virtue of it?" smiled the man behind the counter.

"My old dad wouldn't use anything else for a poultice," replied the customer.

This bark, which, I am told, should be in every household, comes from America. It is the bark of the Red Elm or the Moose Elm, as it is sometimes called. Finely powdered, it makes a gruel as nutritious as that made from oatmeal, and with the added virtue of soothing and healing the stomach. When coarsely ground and made into a poultice, Slippery Elm is the finest remedy in the world, I am told, for ulcers, wounds, chilblains and all inflammation.

While I was talking to the chemist, a porter from Smithfield Market came in to ask for a preparation of herbs for stone in the kidney.

"I've been under a doctor for a year," he said, "but this medicine has done me more good in two weeks than all the medicine I've taken in that time."

"Do you diagnose and prescribe herbs for people?" I asked the chemist.

"Never," he replied. "We never diagnose. Most of our customers know the value of these preparations when they

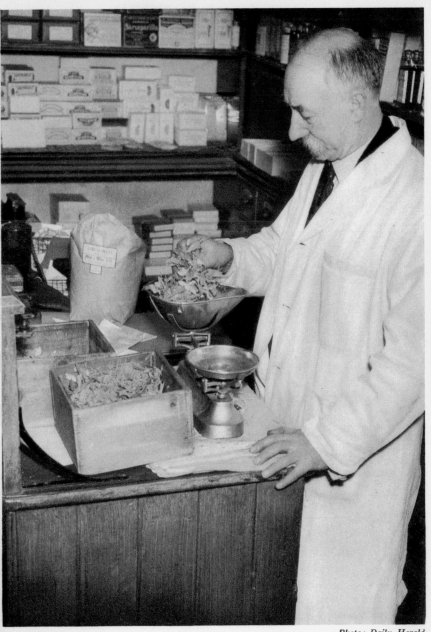

THE HERB SHOP

come to us. If they come and ask us for something to cure biliousness or indigestion, or any definite complaint, we can suggest a remedy. But we never diagnose the complaint."

I picked up a strange assortment of old-fashioned knowledge as I examined the herbarium at the back of the shop. St. John's Bread is a pod about four to eight inches long. You can make a broth from it which was much used by singers in ancient times to improve their voices. The root of Lady's Slipper, powdered and taken in sweetened water, is a nerve tonic, gives sleep, and is useful for headaches and neuralgia.

The root, stem and flowers of lily of the valley (half an ounce to a pint of boiling water) have been used for dropsy and valvular disease of the heart.

Powdered Mistletoe leaves are used for hysteria, epilepsy and blood pressure.

An infusion of powdered Mouse-ear is excellent for whooping cough.

The leaves of the Scarlet Pimpernel are good for dropsy and rheumatic affections, but the potent mixture (ten ounces of Scarlet Pimpernel to one pint of diluted alcohol) must evidently be used with caution.

The root and stem of the Primrose is an ancient remedy for muscular rheumatism, paralysis and gout, but one that is now seldom used.

Rosemary-oil cures headaches, is an excellent stomachic, a nerve tonic and, combined with Borax, prevents premature baldness.

A tea made of Shepherd's Purse is good for all kidney complaints.

Sunflower seeds, good Hollands gin and sugar make a wonderful remedy for coughs, colds and pulmonary affections.

A visit to this thriving "ghost" of London has made me read an old, brown, dog-eared copy of *The English Housewife*, which Gervase Markham wrote in 1649. The sub-title to his book is: "the inward and outward Vertues which ought to be in a compleat Woman."

Among his recipes for all kinds of ailments, which, until I knew of this herb shop, I regarded as concoctions impossible nowadays to obtain, are:

Take the juyce of Lovage and drop it into the eare, and it will cure any venome and kill any worme, earewig or other vermine.

For Griefes in the Stomack: to ease pain in the stomach, take Endine, Mints, of each a like quantity, and steep them in white wine a dayes space; then, straining and adding thereunto a little Cinnamon and Pepper, give it to the sick person to drink, and if you adde thereto a little of the pouder of Horse-mint and Calamint, it will comfort the stomach exceedingly.

Looking through hundreds of ancient remedies of this kind, I found hardly one containing an herb which cannot be procured to-day in Farringdon Street.

But it is not in the realm of medicine, but in that of cookery and the composition of Elizabethan liquors, that the herb shop may appeal to most people. I believe that after a visit to this shop one could make the following Elizabethan cocktail:

To Make Aquavita

Take of Rosemary flowers two handfuls, of Marjoram, Winter-savory, Rosemary, Rew, Time, Germander, Rybworte, Harts-tongue, Mousear, Whitewormewood, Buglosse, Red Sage, Liver-wort, Hoarehound, fine Lavender, Islop-crops, Penny royall, Red fennell, of each one handful: of Elecompane rootes, clean-pared and sliced, two handfuls: then take all these aforesaid and shred them, but not wash them, then take four gallon and more of Strong Ale and one gallon of sack lees, and put all these aforesaid hearbes shred into it, and then put into it one pounde of Licoras bruised, halfe a pound of Aniseeds, cleane, sifted and bruised, and of Mace and Nutmeg bruised, of each one ounce.

Then put together into your stilling-pot, close covered with Rye paste, and make a soft fire under your pot, and as the head of the Limbeck heateth, draw out your hot water and put in cold, but see your fire be not too rash at the first. When the water is distilled take a gallon glasse with a wide mouth and put therein a bottle of the best water and clearest, and put into it a pottle of Rosa solis, halfe a pound of Dates, bruised, and one ounce of grains and half a pound of Sugar, half an ounce of Seede pearle beaten, three leaves of fine gold. Stirre all these together well. Then stoppe your glasse and set it in the sunne the space of one or two months. Then clarify it and use it at your discretion: for a spoonful or two at a time is sufficient.

I am sure that no one will question Markham's warning!
Still, if anyone were brave enough to brew Markham's
"Aquavita," I think the herb shop in Farringdon Street is
probably the only place in London where he could obtain
the ingredients.

CHAPTER

6

CURFEW BELL

One of the facts about English history which every one knows is that the Curfew was decreed by William the Conqueror to lessen the risk of fire in cities built almost entirely of wood. There is, however, a record that the curfew was rung at Oxford in the reign of Alfred the Great, so that the Conqueror may merely have tightened up a regulation already in force.

In Norman times, the Curfew was tolled in London at eight o'clock in the evening by the bell of St. Martin's-le-Grand. This church once stood where the General Post Office now stands. As soon as the first notes rang out, all the other bells began to peal until the City of London rocked with the sound of them.

Those bells could be heard far away among the open fields of Charing to the west, across the marshy Thames to the south, over the moors to the east and among the forests that lay to the north. At the sound all travellers approaching the City spurred their horses into a canter, and those too far off to gain the gates within a reasonable time began to loiter, as they contemplated a night in one of the taverns outside London Wall.

On the first stroke of the bell, the city gates were shut. There were originally only four main gates: Aldgate, on the east; Aldersgate, on the north; Ludgate, on the west; and Bridegate, on the south bank of the Thames. It was possible, however, for travellers to gain entrance after the first notes of the Curfew by the wicket gates, which were not closed until the last note of the warning.

Silence and darkness then settled over London. Fires and lights were quenched; taverns put up their shutters; markets were discontinued and London settled under a gloom deeper than any it was to know for eight centuries when, facing a threat of war from the air, it darkened its windows in the nightly "black-out" of 1939.

It may surprise many Londoners to know that at least four bells continue to ring the Curfew every night. They are the bells of Gray's Inn, Lincoln's Inn, the Tower of London, and the Charterhouse. Every night a bell-ringer grasps the bell-rope as his predecessors have done for over eight centuries, and sends out the message that Norman William desires all fires and lights to be quenched. If there is a more interesting ghost in London than the sound of the Norman Curfew, I have not encountered it.

Why, one wonders, has it been continued? In York, for instance, some one left money for this custom. A mediæval traveller was lost in the Forest of Galtres; as he wandered this way and that, fearing at any moment an attack from wolves, he heard the Curfew ringing in York, and, following the sound of the bell, came safely to Bootham Bar. In thankfulness, he left money for the curfew to be rung in York for ever. In London, however, I know of no such legacies. Our curfews are rung because they have always been rung.

I went down to the Charterhouse about half-past seven one evening to listen to the curfew. At that time of night the cars, which are parked all day in Charterhouse-square, have departed, and the old place, with its gaunt collection of tall plane trees, is the London of two centuries ago.

To pass from this square under the archway of the Charterhouse is, however, to slip still farther back through Time to the England of the sixteenth century. The Charterhouse is a peaceful haven of lawns, cloisters, quadrangles and little courtyards that might be in Oxford.

When the Carthusian monks were driven from this property, it came at length into the possession of Thomas Sutton, a shrewd Elizabethan soldier who, when on service in the north country, had foreseen the commercial possibilities of the Durham coalfield. Coal, and a marriage with an heiress, made Sutton the richest commoner of his time. It was said that his annual income was £5,000 and his capital over £60,000.

Wishing to enter heaven somehow, for he had led an intensely active commercial life, Sutton determined to found a school for poor boys and a retreat for old men who had fallen on bad days. His noble thought has endured. The school, however, is no longer a school for poor boys, but his retreat remains a haven for elderly men who have known better days.

There are sixty-three of them, widowers or bachelors, all of them old soldiers or sailors, or professional men. They live in rooms, attend chapel once a day, dine together in hall, and receive a pension of £1 a week.

Their rooms are full of memories. There is always something in them that forms a link with better times; good books, perhaps an expensive carriage clock, and portraits in silver frames. And every night the sixty-three old men hear the curfew rung from the bell of their chapel. It rings once for every old man in residence. If it should toll only sixty-two times, sixty-two old men would know that one of their

brothers had escaped from the rather wistful beauty of re-
duced circumstances.

The chapel was dark. The bell-rope hung down in the
entrance porch. There was a notice near it warning the bell-
ringer not to ring more than so many times a minute in case
he cracks the bell.

The porter came in, took off his peak cap and his blue coat,
and approached the bell.

"Now you won't speak to me while I'm ringing, will
you?" he asked. "I must get the number right."

He waited until the clock had chimed eight o'clock, then
he grasped the bell-rope.

"One," he said; and far above us came the mellow note of
the Charterhouse curfew.

"Two," he said; and pulled on the rope again.

"Three"; and so on until he had completed the sixty-three.

I thought that this curfew is the only one left in England
that is really a curfew, because now and then, when it misses
a note, it signifies, to all who know the meaning, that a light
has been quenched.

CHAPTER

7

"WHOSE KEYS?"

Something I wrote in a book about London years ago has made the ancient ceremony of "the Keys" well known in this country and in the United States. It was then that I was asked to broadcast this ceremony.

Once a year for several years I used to go down to the Tower of London at night, at the request of 2LO—as Broadcasting House then was—and, from the chilly gloom of the

Byward Tower, speak the introduction to the ceremony of
the Keys. I always enjoyed that strange adventure in the
Tower at night.

The microphone was generally balanced on a tin kettle
set in some queer niche at the bottom of a flight of spiral
stairs. Cloaked Warders would tiptoe into the old guard-
room under the mistaken impression that the microphone
was "live," often upsetting a box or tripping over a cable
with a hearty but uncompleted oath.

With the wind whistling into the old tower, I would stand
shivering, with coat-collar turned up, waiting for the moment when an engineer, with earphones strapped to his head,
would make wide, noiseless mouths, the signal for me to
begin in a strange, unnatural voice, "I am speaking to you
from the Tower of London."

I always wondered whether people really believed me!

The nightly ceremony of "the Keys" is, in many ways,
the most remarkable ghost in London. Of all the seemingly
weird appointments that London makes with its past, this
nightly function in His Majesty's Tower is, in my opinion,
the most interesting.

The Tower is not only one of the most ancient buildings
in use in England, but it is the only fortress that has been in
continuous occupation for over eight and a half centuries.
The function of the Tower to-day is the same as it was when
William the Conqueror founded it eleven years after the
Battle of Hastings.

It is still a royal palace. It is still a garrison and an armoury. During the last War we saw how this grey old building resumed its tragic function as a prison and a place that can still deal death to traitors; and that, no doubt, is its function once again.

In the old days it was the custom of kings to perpetuate the royal connection with the Tower by spending the night before the coronation within its walls. Once in history a king moved to the safety of its walls during a rebellion. That was when Henry VII took up residence in the Tower when Perkin Warbeck, backed by France and Scotland, was pretending to be one of the princes murdered in the Tower and the rightful heir to the Throne.

To-day, however, the only outward symbol connecting the Tower of London with the King is the fact that the password to the Tower after dark is still, in theory, known only to His Majesty and to the Lord Mayor of London. Every quarter a list is issued giving the password necessary for every night of the following three months.

It is a fact that once the Tower gates are locked at night, no one without the password can gain admission. Even within the Tower after dark the sentries challenge those who move about.

Nobody knows when or how the curious old ceremony of parading the "King's Keys" was first observed. The earliest record of it is in the reign of Edward III, when a certain John of London performed the ceremony, but the custom

CEREMONY OF THE KEYS, THE TOWER OF LONDON

was probably a commonplace of Tower routine centuries before that time.

It is, I think, one of the most impressive ceremonies I know, made so, no doubt, by its antiquity, by romantic surroundings, and by the fact that it takes place in private.

Shortly before ten at night the Chief Warder comes into the guard-room. He puts on his long red cloak and his Tudor bonnet, and he takes down a lantern containing a tallow candle. When the light is burning, he picks up the Keys of the Wicket Gate and the Byward Tower and, walking to the main guard, calls for an "escort for the Keys."

One N.C.O. and four men fall in with rifles and fixed bayonets. The Chief Warder, with his lantern and the Keys, places himself in the centre, and off they march towards the Wicket Gate on Tower Hill. At ordinary times the Chief Warder, meeting an officer, would salute him, but when he carries the Keys an officer salutes him—or rather the Keys. As they march along, every sentry on the way to the main gates comes to attention and presents arms. Civilians encountered on the march stand still and lift their hats.

First the Wicket Gate, by which sightseers enter the Tower, is locked, and then the escort and the Keys retrace their steps to the towers of the Outer Ward.

There is a great clanging of metal as the ancient bolts are shot home. The old gates are locked, leaving only the small postern open at the side.

When, however, the escort and the Keys come to the dark arch of the Bloody Tower, the sentry steps out, lowers the point of his bayonet, and challenges: "Halt! Who comes there?"

"The Keys," cries the Chief Warder.

"Whose Keys?"

"King George's Keys!" cries the Chief Warder.

"Pass, King George's Keys. All's well," cries the sentry; and the escort passes up the slight rise of ground under the Bloody Tower towards the guard-room, where the main guard is drawn up under an officer.

The guard presents arms, the Warder steps forward with his lantern, lifts his bonnet and cries: "God Preserve King George."

The guard, from officer to drummer-boy, answers: "Amen."

I would like to know the origin of the challenge at the Bloody Tower. It is such an absurd question that I feel sure that it must have an interesting history.

They tell a funny story about this challenge in the Tower, but whether it is true or not I cannot say. It is said that during the last War a line regiment which took over the Tower from the Guards was eager to make a good show of the ancient ceremony of "the Keys."

The sentries were carefully rehearsed and the great moment came. Everything went off splendidly until the escort was halted before the Bloody Tower.

"WHOSE KEYS?"

"Halt!" cried the sentry. "Who goes there?"

"The Keys!" cried the Chief Warder dramatically.

Then followed an unhappy silence.

"Go on, you fool, say 'Whose Keys?'" hissed the usual watchful sergeant-major; but the sentry remained stubbornly dumb.

"What's the matter with you, my lad? Say 'Whose Keys?'" pressed the authorities, and at length the sentry was heard to remark:

"All right—*I'll bite* . . . Whose Keys?"

Alas, this story is probably too good to be true!

CHAPTER
8

AN ORDINARY

It was once the custom of those travellers and business men who ate away from their own homes to patronize what was known as "an ordinary." The word, when applied to something that is habitual, is very ancient. We still have the term, "an ambassador in ordinary," to describe an ambassador who is constantly in residence in a foreign country, and "physician in ordinary," to describe a doctor who is always in attendance on the monarch.

The "ordinary," however, which our ancestors patronized when they were hungry, denoted a public meal served at a tavern at a given time and at a fixed price; and in the old days every other tavern in the City of London specialized in "an ordinary."

In the reign of Queen Anne there seem to have been "ordinaries" for every purse. We read of a "Fivepenny Ordinary," and even of a "Twopenny Ordinary." I suppose the modern substitute for the old-fashioned "ordinary" is the four- or five-course table d'hôte made popular by the restaurants of Soho.

One of the last real old-fashioned "ordinaries" in the country—and certainly the last one to be observed with due state in London—takes place every day sharp at 1 o'clock in the tavern which used to be called the "Queen's Arms," in Bird in Hand Court, off Cheapside.

This is a curious and attractive little court. Even rebuilding operations and modern shops cannot quite rob it of the secret and romantic air which it inherits from the eighteenth century. It is still essentially the same court that Keats saw when he sat in his lodgings there and wrote "On First Looking into Chapman's Homer." At the end of the court is the ripe-looking tavern which still offers a "Two Shilling Fish Ordinary."

This meal is a genuine survival from a former age. I believe that there is a more or less unbroken history linking it with fish dinners that began in the year 1723 at "The Three Tons," in Bell Alley, near Billingsgate.

Those were provided by an innkeeper named Simpson, and they rapidly became popular. Simpson eventually sold his business, when he judged it time to retire, and entered into a bond for £500 not to open up a similar business within a specified area. Finding, however, that he could not be happy in retirement, he paid down his £500, bought the "Queen's Arms," and ran it on the same lines as the old tavern in Bell Alley. His "Two Shilling Fish Ordinary" is one of the few things that have not gone up in price since 1914.

I went to Simpson's on a Friday, and was shown into a brown, experienced-looking apartment on an upper floor, where a large horse-shoe table was set for about fifty guests.

There were three throne-like chairs at the head of the table. I was told that they were occupied by the chairman and his two chief guests. I was told also that they are made of wood rescued from the tavern during a fire in 1898.

The wall space above the Chairman's throne was covered with framed certificates on which I read the names of guests who had successfully guessed the weight, height and girth of a huge cheese, a competition that is carried out once a week to conclude the feast. This solemn problem is solved so rarely that the proprietor, in order to celebrate a successful guess, serves the whole company with champagne.

While I admired the good, ripe old room, sanctified by so many years of honest English food and so much jolly English humour, the other guests began to arrive, most of them city men and regular habitués; and a few of them curious sightseers like myself.

For nearly two centuries the "Fish Ordinary" fought desperately against the inclusion of women, but about seventeen years ago the stronghold fell, and now women sit down every day with the men.

The earliest to arrive was an old man in a black overcoat and a silk hat. He had twinkling blue eyes and a snow-white imperial. He was the Chairman. As he took his seat a waiter handed him a black apron, which he carefully tied round his waist. He then cast an experienced eye at the huge carving-knife before him, and at the shining battery of soup-ladles and fish-servers. When we were all seated he said grace, and a huge tureen of soup was carried in.

The Chairman ladled out the soup. The plates were handed from guest to guest. The soup was followed by a mighty dish of stewed eels.

The Chairman again served his enormous family. The eels were followed by fried plaice. He portioned one fillet to each person.

Every time a new dish came on and the dirty plates were removed, one could tell the novices, because they were willing to relinquish their used fish-knives and forks. This is not done at a "Fish Ordinary"! You use the same knife and fork

for all three courses, as, in fact, you do to-day all over Spain
and in the country districts of France.

What a lot of good humour and friendliness, I thought,
has departed from the everyday things of life. Only a century ago these merry family meetings round a table were
daily events in a thousand taverns.

It was customary for one man to act the part of host and
to take pride in serving the guests, in upholding the dignity
of the "chair," and in making a joke now and then.

This, the Chairman often did, first banging the table with
a wooden hammer. Mr. Vice, from the end of the horse-
shoe, shouted, "Chair! Gentlemen, please!"; and in the silence that followed, our Chairman, who was over eighty
years of age, rose to his feet and told us a story.

When the last whitebait had been eaten, a four-foot long
roly-poly pudding was carried before the Chairman, who
neatly cut it into portions and, ladling hot syrup over it,
sent it on its way.

Meanwhile a wooden stand formed of oak from Nelson's
Victory was placed at the head table. Two waiters then appeared bearing a colossal Cheshire cheese. Slices were sent
round accompanied by printed slips of paper.

"Now ladies and gentlemen," said the Chairman, "we
will first guess the height of the cheese."

We regarded the mountain thoughtfully and wrote down
our guesses. The Chairman measured the height and an-
nounced the dimension. Three visitors were found to have

been correct. We next guessed the girth of the cheese.

A thrill of excitement went round when it was discovered that a man sitting near the cheese, who had already success-fully written down the height, had also guessed the girth.

"Put the champagne on ice!" called the Chairman.

But, alas, our champion failed on the weight! He was half a pound out! Someone whispered to me that he had been guessing every week for ten years and had never quite got it right.

The great cheese was carried away, the guests pushed back their chairs and, with a friendly nod to the Chairman, or a handshake, went back to their business.

I left them with the feeling that there is still one place in London where the leisurely good nature of a past age lingers a little while each day.

CHAPTER

9

HANSOM CAB

Sitting beside the coal fire in his bed-sitting-room at New-ington Butts, Mr. Frisbee extended towards the blaze a foot in a carpet slipper and described the sound of gold coins falling on a London pavement.

"There's a funny ring about gold," he said. "A blind man could tell a falling sovereign from a shilling. But perhaps you've never heard the sound sovereigns make when they fall on a pavement—fifty jimmy-o'-goblins coming down like hail?"

"No, never."

"And you never will," commented Mr. Frisbee, "for the days when the toffs and the mashers used to chuck their money about is gone, finally and for ever. There isn't any money to chuck about to-day.

"Mind you, forty years ago there were greater extremes of poverty and riches, but, on the whole, everything was cheaper and men were jollier, if you know what I mean.

"It's the fashion to-day to talk about the 'naughty 'nineties.' Well, it's true London wasn't exactly a girls' school forty years ago, but I'm sure that, so far as naughtiness goes, we weren't worse than modern London. Why, bless my soul! . . . but what was I talking about? Oh, I know—golden sovereigns on the pavement.

"Now you wouldn't hardly believe what I am going to tell you; but it's a fact. It was one summer's morning, very early. The sun was just up. A lovely morning. I was standing with my cab outside a famous nightclub that used to be in Regent Street. Out came a toff in full evening-dress. He put his hand in his pocket and said: 'Boys, do you want a scramble?' And with that he ups with his hand—like this—and down came a shower of golden sovereigns!

"Well, I tell you, in a second every driver was down from his cab and every street lounger was joining in the wildest scramble you ever saw. And when they'd picked them-

selves up, down came another shower. More than fifty sov-
ereigns were picked up off Regent Street that morning.
Then the toff says: 'It's all finished, boys. I've got no more.
Take me home.'

"Of course, it was a different world: a world of horses.
Horses and drink always go together, I think. That's funny,
isn't it? But it's true. On cold mornings when we'd been
standing in Leicester Square, six of us would go into the
Continental when it opened at 5 o'clock and start the day
with a pint of rum and a jug of hot water."

That is the way Mr. Albert Frisbee reviews the dead
splendours of the last century as he sits by his fire at New-
ington Butts. Mr. Frisbee is one of the last three hansom
cab-drivers in London. He was driving a hansom forty years
ago, when there were over fifteen thousand horse-cabs and
hansoms on the streets of London. His old badge number
is 14,037. Most nights at about eight-thirty he takes up a
position in Piccadilly, and, sitting high on his perch with his
whip in a slot beside him, waits there like the last ghost of
Victorian London.

Who rides in his hansom cab these days? He will tell
you that he trades on curiosity and sentiment.

The curious go to him as they would go in a sedan-chair,
just to be able to say that they have ridden in a hansom
cab. Sometimes people in love think it is a romantic thing
to do. Sometimes people who have had too much to drink

consider it rather comic to drive about in such a strange vehicle.

Mr. Frisbee (who remembers what it felt like to be told to drive like blazes to Hounslow) regards with a bleak eye those revellers who treat the last hansom as a joke.

But there are other fares. Now and then an old man will wave impatiently from the kerb and cry, "Hi, cabby," and Mr. Frisbee knows that he is about to drive someone who remembers what London was like before the Boer War. Those old men cannot resist the hansom in Piccadilly. Ghost calls to ghost.

They climb in, close the apron and sit back, hoping, perhaps, that the tall wheels will catch up with some memory which even the swiftest car could never overtake.

I asked Mr. Frisbee if he could buy six hansoms anywhere to-day, and he shook his head.

"Not for all the gold in the Bank," he replied.

All those thousands of "London gondolas" have vanished in our time. The taxicab, slowly at first, and then swiftly, drove them from the streets.

"There used to be a tale," said Mr. Frisbee, "that somewhere at Hendon all the thousands of hansom cabs were lying in a huge dump, waiting to be broken up. And I believe it was a true story. That's what happened to them. They were sold for one pound and two pounds apiece. They were broken up for the glass, the springs and the woodwork."

Then Mr. Frisbee told me how difficult it is in London to-day to find a spare part for a hansom cab.

"No one knows how to make them to-day," he said. "The building of a hansom is a lost art. The other day, when I needed a new pump-shaft, I couldn't find a man anywhere in the trade who was able to cut one for me. At last I tracked down a man who used to make them. He was eighty years old and retired. After a bit of persuasion he did the job."

Horses? Mr. Frisbee's eyes light up when he remembers the kind of horses he used to drive forty years ago.

"Every one understood horses in those days and you couldn't get a fare if you had a crock between the shafts. We were prouder of our horses than any man can be of the finest car. You ought to have seen us racing down the Embankment from the City in the evening, with the mud flying back over the cabs on wet days. We used to call the Embankment 'the race-course.' I remember once . . ."

And Mr. Frisbee is off again at a gallop.

In Mr. Frisbee's hansom, and those of his companions, Mr. Lamont and Mr. Woolf, we see the last representatives of a vehicle more notable in its time than the taxicab is in ours. The taxicab is universal: the hansom belonged to London.

It was originally the invention of an architect, Joseph Aloysius Hansom, who was born at York in 1803. He sold the rights to his "patent safety cab" in 1834 to a company for £10,000; but the company never paid, and all he received for his invention was £300.

He was an unfortunate man. He designed and built the Birmingham Town Hall, but the transaction, owing to a reckless agreement, caused his bankruptcy. More enduring memorials of Hansom than his cab are St. Walpurge's Church at Preston, Lancashire, the Catholic Cathedral in Plymouth, the Jesuit College in Manchester, and the Church of St. Philip Neri at Arundel.

It must have seemed to Hansom—for he died in his eightieth year, long before the coming of the motor-car—that his invention was fated to go on for ever, an unhappy reminder of the fortune that he might have made. In his most inventive moments, however, he could never have foreseen a day when the last hansom would ply for hire in Piccadilly like the ghost of a dead age.

And Mr. Frisbee, with his abundant memories of "toffs" and spilt sovereigns—he, too, is a fitting coachman for this ghostly gondola.

THE LAMPLIGHTER

The lamplighter, with his pole on his shoulder, is already among the ghosts of London. Sometimes, when I look from my window in the evening, I see him emerge from a side street and disappear beneath an old archway.

He is more than ever like a ghost, because there is not a lamp in sight that he could reach with his pole, were it ten times as long. Those lamps are all tall, modern lamps that are lit up by time-clocks or from a main. Still, the lamplighter crosses this street in the evening on some mysterious mission.

I wonder how many people feel, as I do, an affection for lamplighters that dates from the earliest years of childhood. I remember what it felt like to wait, pressing my face against a window-pane, for the moment when he would come with a leisurely stride, leaving little stars and pools of yellow light behind him; and what a lovely moment it was when he would pause opposite to lift his pole and bring the lamp to life.

In bed at night in a silent house, the memory of that little pool of gold was somehow infinitely consoling before one fell asleep, and, in the stillness of a night of ugly dreams, what could be more comforting than to hop out of bed and see the lamp burning there, so still and calm, so brave in the dark?

Robert Louis Stevenson is the only poet who has remembered how romantic a lamplighter could be to a child watching for him at the window; and every time I read his *Child's Garden of Verses* I am a small boy again, with my eyes on the window.

For we are very lucky with a lamp before the door,
And Leerie stops to light it as he lights so many more;
And O! before you hurry by with ladder and with light,
O Leerie, see a little child and nod to him to-night.

As I was walking the other evening in a street not far from Westminster Abbey, I saw twelve men approach a shed and draw from it, one after the other, lamplighter's poles. I watched them with some curiosity for I had not seen such a sight for years. They took my mind back to a time when every street had its lamplighter. Twelve Leeries with their poles across their shoulders setting out to light the lamps of London!

"There's not many of us stick lighters left," one of them told me. "Most of the lamps nowadays are turned on automatically. But, here and there, a few of us still muster of an evening. Yes, 'muster's' the name we give it. They've changed the lamps, the torches we carry, the standards, the system of booking, and pretty well everything, but the old-fashioned muster still goes on. We're the last of the old brigade."

"How long have you been lighting lamps?" I asked him.

"I'm one of the few left who used to light the old flat-flamed burners, and they were done away with about thirty-five years ago. I can remember Fulham being lit with flat flames. I remember, too, what it was like to light them. You tipped your lever up and your by-pass touched the gas, but —what a rotten light it was, although we thought it wonderful in those days!

"Thieves could knock you down and get away between this lamp and the next. Terrible rough times they were, those old days! I remember Tufton Street, Westminster, when it was a regular bear garden and you never liked to go down it of a Friday with your pay in your pocket. Lumme, the fights I've seen down there! There was one Sunday they called 'Bloody Sunday'; and it was, too.

"But I must be getting along. It gets dark so quickly this time of year. I light my lamps about four o'clock, and I'm up at about six to put them out in the morning. Of course it gets later and earlier, if you know what I mean."

"How many lamps do you light?"

"A hundred and twenty. Great George Street, Petty France, Queen Anne's Gate, and all round there. It's about a five mile walk night and morning. . . ."

And "Mr. Leerie" shouldered his torch and set off into the February dusk.

He interested me so much that I went to the offices of the Gas Light and Coke Company in the Horseferry Road, and asked some questions about lamplighters. This company has been supplying gas to London since 1812, when gas was regarded by many as an invention of the devil.

Londoners may be surprised to know that a number of the most famous streets in the city are lit, not by electricity, but by gas. Whitehall, Pall Mall, Parliament Square, Regent Street, Piccadilly (from the Circus to Albemarle Street), Victoria Street, are all gas-lit. Chelsea is a stronghold of gas. The company supplies gas to six counties and deals with eighty-four municipal authorities. The official who greeted me in the Horseferry Road pointed to a map of his area and told me that his first lamp was at Windsor and his last within half a mile of the sea at Shoeburyness.

I wish all big business contained men with his sense of history and romance.

In ten minutes we were talking about the history of gas, discussing Rowlandson's skits on the first gas-lamps, laughing at the sermons which parsons preached against gas, and then, by leaps and bounds, we approached modern gas, at which point my friend showered publicity handbooks on me, told me how much better gas was than electricity, edging his chair nearer and nearer, his eyes blazing with such fervid conviction that, at the end of it, I was almost willing to ask for a corps of men to tear down my wretched electric lights and install gas instead. At this point, I think, we fortunately went out to lunch.

After lunch I amassed an enormous and variegated mass of information about gas. I began to feel mentally gassed. My head was within the oven of his enthusiasm, but, by a supreme effort of will, I managed to take a breath of air and shout: "I want to know about lamplighters!"

"Lamplighters?" he cried. "Whatever do you want to know about lamplighters for? Never mind, I'll tell you about them."

He consulted some papers from a drawer of his desk: "There are," he said, "four hundred and twelve stick lamplighters left, but not all of them in London. Of this number,

Photo: The Times

THE LAMPLIGHTER

thirty-one are men who used to light the old fish-tail, flat-flame burners. They work hard and they are very good fellows. They have to clean the lamps as well as light them. There are stick lighters who light lamps with torches, and there are clock lighters who set the automatic clocks that regulate the lamps. The stick lighters think the clock men have the better job; but it's a matter of opinion.

"Now the old-fashioned stick lighter is gradually being superseded by the clock lighter, and you are quite right when you call the stick lighter a ghost of London. He is a vanishing type. He was always a popular character in the old days; and still is so, when anybody notices him. One old lamplighter told me that he always gets a pound of pork sausages at Christmas-time from a butcher on his beat, and another one told me that certain houses never forget him on Boxing Day. That is a relic of the old times. That's all I can tell you about lamplighters."

I was about to thank him, but he wagged a finger at me and went on:

"Now if you really want to see some queer ghosts of London, come with me. I guarantee to show you some things that few people know anything about. Did you know, for instance, that the base of one lamp-post in London is an old ship's cannon? No. I thought you didn't! Are you ready?"

I had some vague intention of putting him off, but, catching the crusading fire in his eye, I meekly followed him.

CHAPTER

11

ANCIENT LIGHTS

The official of the Gas Light and Coke Company, whose terrific enthusiasm I have endeavoured to indicate, led me to the Horseferry Road, where his car was standing.

"Jump in," he said. "We're going first to the Albert Hall."

Just inside Hyde Park he suddenly stopped and leapt out of the car. We approached the two tall lamp standards

that rise just inside the park gates, and are matched by a row
of companion standards outside the gates on the pavement.

"Some of the earliest standards in London," he cried,
giving them a slap with his hand. "Lovely stuff! Put up
about 1831, in the reign of William IV. There are not many
about now; a few round Carlton House Terrace, but that's
all. Good old standards, aren't they? Doing their job faithfully for over a century, and as good as new. See that W
there, stamped in metal? That's all that is left of 'W.R. IV.'
—William Rex Four, you know. On the standards outside
I think you can still see a complete IV, but the royal mono-
gram has worn away.

"Ah, ghosts of London," he cried, patting the lamp standards tenderly. "What ghosts of London! What sights they've
seen, standing here for a hundred years! Imagine the light
shining on faces now dead and gone, the faces of lovers in
the park! Just think of that. Girls in poke bonnets and fellows with Dundreary whiskers. That's romance, that is!
You can write a story about that. Burning gas all that time,
gaslight shining down—not electricity—GAS!"

In the presence of an enthusiasm greater than my own I
always feel a trifle uneasy, so I followed him back to the
car with a feeling of relief.

He turned out of the Park and ran down Queen's Gate,
where he pointed out a line of lamp posts on the left-hand
side as you go towards Cromwell Road.

"Queer standards, those," he cried, "nobody knows anything about them. They're a different pattern from any in London. They're only on one side of the street and there are only a few of them. We can't match them. We try to patch them up, but when they get too old they have to go. Many's the time I've wondered where they came from. It's my belief, although I've no reason for saying so, that they are a relic of the Great Exhibition of 1851."

We took the first turning to the left out of Queen's Gate, which is a short, wide road called Prince Consort Road.

"Do you notice anything about it?" asked my friend.

"Yes, I do," I said, "I notice a lot of lamps."

"Got it, first time!" he cried approvingly. "This is the best-lit street in London, yet nobody knows anything about it. It is one of the quietest too, after dark. You can see there are no houses in it, only a hostel for students, the College of Music, and a few big buildings. But look at the lamps! Look at them! There are twice as many lamps in this short street as in any other of the same size in London. Now, why is it?"

"I don't know."

"Well, I'll tell you. Here's another ghost of London for you! Long ago, when this road was hardly lit at all, a young man whose family lived in Queen's Gate was run over and killed in this road by a horse and carriage. The coroner stated at the inquest that the accident had been partly due to the bad lighting of Prince Consort Road.

"Now, when the boy's mother died, she left money in her

will to the local parish for the better lighting of the road. It's quite unnecessary—with gas as good as it is now; but still this road, which is deserted after dark, is the best lit road in London. I'll bet you that no one, except perhaps the policeman on the beat, knows that story.

"What a ghost of London! The gaslight shining down every night, a kind of memorial. Queer place London, isn't it? Little odd bits of romance and pathos everywhere, if you only keep your eyes open. Now we'll go to Trafalgar Square, where I'll show you a few more ghosts."

He rushed on to Trafalgar Square. We parked the car somewhere in a side-street, and dodged across the traffic to the square.

First we stood in front of the National Gallery, where my friend pointed out two peculiar octagonal lanterns on bronze standards. We then walked round to the front of the square, where at each end, mounted on two squat towers, are two slightly larger lanterns of the same type.

"You'll never guess what those are," said my friend. "Thousands upon thousands of people pass them every day and don't know what they are. Those four glass lamps are old oil lamps from Nelson's *Victory*. Our lamplighters and cleaners call them the 'Battle Lamps.' They get extra pay for cleaning them. And it's an awful job! There's a ghost of London for you, bang in the middle of everything—the lamps that swung on Nelson's flagship when she went into battle at Trafalgar!"

Our next call was in St. James's Square. We stopped opposite the head office of the Canada Life Assurance Company at No. 2. This used to be the town house of Lord Falmouth. My friend asked me to look at the lamp-post that
stood in the pavement opposite the door. It was a short, fat,
metal standard about three to four feet in height, and from
the top of it sprang a slender modern lamp standard.

"Now that lamp is unique in London," he said. "It is a
French cannon. Until a few months ago even we of the Gas
Company did not know anything about it. But it became
necessary for us to take up the lamps in St. James's Square.
When we did so, we discovered with surprise that this one
was not a lamp stand at all, but a cannon sunk in the pavement. I'll give you a photograph taken at the time, which
shows how half of it, up to the trunnions, was buried out
of sight and how the lamp bracket was stuck in the muzzle.

"We made inquiries and discovered an interesting story.
In May, 1747, the great seaman, who afterwards became
Admiral Edward Boscawen, was in command of a 74-gun
ship called the *Namur*. He was a brother of Lord Falmouth.
This ship played her part in the tremendous victory over
the French off Cape Finisterre, and this London lamp-post
was one of the guns which she captured from the French.
Boscawen presented it to his brother, and, when gas lighting
came in about sixty years later, the old cannon was used as
the stand for the first gas light in front of Lord Falmouth's
house. Of course, we put it back in position. The lamp stand-

THE CANNON LAMP-POST, ST. JAMES'S SQUARE

ard springs from the muzzle that once fired shot at An-
son's squadron one hundred and eighty-eight years ago."

The gas enthusiast turned his eager face to me: "Have I
shown you ghosts of London?" he asked.

"You have," I said, "and you have also given me one of
the most breathless hours I have ever spent in London."

"I'm glad," he replied, "and if there's anything you ever
want to know about gas—come to me! Gas, mind, not electricity! Gas. There's romance in gas. There's history in gas.
Gas is the best illuminant, the cheapest, and you never get
black-outs with it. Give me gas every time!"

With a cheery wave of his accomplished hand he was off
and away.

CHAPTER

12

"ORDER, ORDER!"

No story about the ghosts of London would be complete without some mention of the strange ancient spectres which haunt the daily life of Parliament. Whenever the cry of "Order!" or "Privilege!" is raised in the House of Commons, you can be sure that some unfortunate Member has, perhaps innocently, walked through one of the venerable phantoms.

The Houses of Parliament stand on part of the land once

occupied by the Palace of Westminster. This building was an extraordinary collection of halls and courtyards, and was occupied as a royal palace as early as the time of Canute. William the Conqueror added to this palace, Rufus built the magnificent Westminster Hall, which still stands, and for centuries those buildings were the home of English kings.

Parliament naturally gathered near the palace, meeting first in the Chapter House of the Abbey Church, but in 1547 it was moved to St. Stephen's Chapel, within the precincts of the palace. It was enacted by Parliament in the time of Henry VIII that all these premises should be called the King's Palace at Westminster, and be so called for ever.

When, however, the Palace of Westminster was damaged by fire, Henry VIII—that great estate agent—profiting by Cardinal Wolsey's downfall, seized York Place and rebuilt it as the Palace at Whitehall, which then became the chief seat of the English court, and so remained through Tudor and Stuart times, until a fire destroyed it. St. James's Palace was then brought into prominence as the court of the Hanoverians.

Through all these changes, Parliament continued to meet in its old place among the relics of the ancient Palace of Whitehall. This was burnt down in 1834 and nothing remains of it now except Westminster Hall and the crypt of the Chapel of St. Stephen, called St. Mary Undercroft.

The present Houses of Parliament, built in 1840–67,

cover the site of the old royal residences, and the present narrow entrance to the Central Hall, called St. Stephen's Hall, exactly corresponds to the ground plan of the vanished St. Stephen's Chapel, in which the Commons met for two hundred and eighty-seven years. Brass studs in the floor mark the site of the Speaker's Chair and the site of the table.

A ghost of those old times survives in the name "St. Stephen's," often used as an equivalent for the House of Commons, and also in the privilege which Members possess of marrying or christening their children in the crypt beneath the hall; and in the habit of Members who bow to the Chair whenever they pass the Speaker, a custom which began, not as a courtesy to the Speaker, but in Catholic days as a genuflection to the altar of the chapel.

An ancient enactment of Henry VIII's time is still in force and the Houses of Parliament are still technically a royal palace. I have been told, and I can well believe it, that certain pundits in Government departments make a point of addressing their letters, when the House is not in session, to "H.M. Palace of Westminster."

Although no king has lived in the Palace of Westminster since Henry VIII, the buildings are still in the custody of a royal official: the hereditary Lord Great Chamberlain, who should not be confused with the Lord Chamberlain of the Household. This officer retains authority over both the Houses of Parliament, although I do not think that there is any way in which he could exercise it unless the monarch decided to sleep there.

George IV spent the night there before his coronation in the Abbey. By ancient tradition the king, if he sleeps at Westminster, must occupy the house of the Lord Great Chamberlain. As this official has now no house there, the difficulty was ingeniously solved in the time of George IV, when the Speaker let his house for one night, at a nominal rent, to the Lord Great Chamberlain.

The *Gentleman's Magazine* for July, 1821, tells us that King and Courtiers spent a restless night. The Deputy Lord Great Chamberlain and his secretary stood on one side of the bed, and the Gentleman Usher of the Black Rod on the other; and there they remained until morning. But the ghosts of Westminster had been appeased!

The Speaker's position is one that is hedged about with many spectres of tradition. It has been excellently said that while the Premier can do no right, the Speaker can do no wrong. He shares with judges an assumption of infallibility.

It is, perhaps, curious that a man who makes no speeches should be called the Speaker. His title, however, refers to his historic position as the spokesman for the Commons: the intermediary between the Commons and the Crown. While the Speaker is an absolute autocrat in the House, he is also its servant. His voice and his eyes are those of the Commons, and this function was memorably defined by Speaker Lenthall when, in a dramatic and fateful moment in English history, Charles I forced his way into the House of Commons and, striding to the Speaker's Chair, demanded the arrest of five Members. In dead silence Charles asked where the five men were sitting. Lenthall replied that he did not know because, as his eyes were controlled by the House, he had "neither eyes to see nor tongue to speak but as the House is pleased to direct."

Since 1688 the Speaker has been termed the First Commoner of the Realm, and the House is not properly constituted unless he is present with the Mace on the table in front of him. He is, with the exception of the King, the only person who can hold a levée, and a symbol of his grandeur was last admired by London crowds during the Coronation Procession of King George VI, when a pair of competent-looking dray horses came along, drawing a heavy old coach evidently constructed before the invention of carriage springs. The Speaker's Coach was built in Holland about 1689 for William of Orange, and I am told on the best authority that its weight is about two tons and fifteen hundredweight, a load much too heavy for ordinary carriage horses. Thus it is that, on those rare occasions when the Speaker goes abroad in state, it is necessary to call in the services of two massive animals who normally spend their lives pulling casks of beer round London.

One of the most powerful symbols in the country is the Mace, which is carried before the Speaker by the Sergeant-at-Arms. When it is under the table the House is in Committee; when it is upon the table the House is sitting.

In stormy times in the past, attempts have been made to bring a sitting to a standstill by the forcible removal of the Mace, and on one occasion, when the Mace was not available, the House had to wait for its arrival before business could be transacted.

This occurred in the middle of the last century, on the day of a naval review at Spithead. Parliament had been adjourned for the day so that Members might attend the review, but the House was timed to sit again at ten that night.

When ten o'clock came, however, there was no Mace. It happened that the train bringing Members of the House back to London was running in two sections, and the official who had the key of the Mace cupboard was travelling in the second section. This train was an hour late. But the House of Commons waited for it, postponing its sitting until after 11 o'clock, when the Mace was at length produced and placed on the table.

Some of the customs of Parliament are persistent ghosts of the old struggle between the Commons and the Crown. Although the Prince of Wales may sit in the House of Commons and listen to debates, that place is the one spot in the royal dominions into which he may not go when he becomes king. In her long reign of over sixty-two years, Queen Victoria never once entered the House of Commons.

A relic of the old struggle is the custom, always jealously observed, of shutting the doors of the Commons in the face of a messenger from the Sovereign. This always occurs at the opening of Parliament. The Gentleman Usher of the Black Rod is commanded by the King to summon the Commons. He makes his way from the House of Lords to the House of Commons, where cries of "Way for Black Rod" clear a passage for him, for it is an ancient regulation that the journey must not be impeded.

As soon as he approaches, the doors of the Commons are shut and bolted in his face. Black Rod then knocks three times. When the sound of his knocking is heard, a delightful little Parliamentary fiction is observed by the Sergeant-at-Arms and the Speaker.

The Sergeant-at-Arms looks up in surprise. "Who can that possibly be?" he seems to say. He looks for guidance to the Speaker. The Speaker gives a solemn nod of his head, and the Sergeant-at-Arms rises and unbolts the door. Every time this amusing pantomime is acted, one can picture the ghosts of those commoners who fought for the privileges of Parliament chuckling in the shades with approval and delight.

There are other ghosts in Parliament. A Member speaking from the front benches must take care not to advance his foot beyond a certain red line on the carpet. This line represents the limit supposed to keep him beyond sword reach of the benches opposite.

A terrible sin against the tradition of a free Parliament would be committed by a Member who locked a door in the House of Commons. One shudders to imagine such an act! In this custom one can perceive the cloaked and hooded ghosts of plotters like Guy Fawkes.

There is, also, a certain portion of the House which is considered to be outside the House, and a Member must be careful not to address the Commons from outside. This barrier is the Boar of the House, to which Sheriffs come with their petitions, and to which offending Members of Parliament are brought to receive the reprimand of the assembly.

Another ghost is the cry "Who goes home?" It echoes through the corridors when the House rises. This cry is a ghost of a London full of footpads and thieves, and of a time when Members of Parliament banded together to walk through the dark streets for the sake of safety.

These are only a few of the ghosts that haunt an assembly as ancient as the House of Commons.

CHAPTER
13

---

*ELY PLACE: TWELVE O'CLOCK
AND ALL'S WELL*

A night-watchman with his coat of many capes, his beaver hat, and his lantern on a pole, is one of the unfailing figures of the Christmas season. He appears romantically on Christmas cards and on the covers of those ecstatically frost-bound periodicals which are, alas, composed in the heat of the preceding summer.

It is not uncommon for most periods in history to idealize

the age of its grandfathers. Such times are just far enough away to appear rather cloudy and interesting, and they are not sufficiently close to inspire the fatuous superiority with which the younger generation so often observes its immediate elders.

How we, for instance, idealize the stage-coach, although, if we read Surtees and one or two heart-felt productions such as Westmacott's *Points of Misery,* we realize what a painful and dreary mode of travelling it must have been: the cold outside, the fetid air inside, the jolts, the swaying, the toll-gates, the hasty descent at all hours in wayside inns for tepid soup and cold mutton, and the guard touting round the table for tips.

Yet, when we see a print of the London to Dover Mail going full gallop, the leaders with their heads in the air, and the red wheels flying, it is impossible not to think that it would have been good to make that journey, at least once, on an outside seat over the boot.

But by what process of the imagination the watchman, or "Charlie," has been idealized it is difficult to understand. He was an unsatisfactory guardian of the public safety. He was often asleep in his box, or trembling in the shadow of it, while the murder was being committed; and some of those who knew him well have suggested that he sometimes had a share of the swag after a robbery.

Through the nepotism, or the plain foolishness, of the parochial authorities who were responsible for the election of the Watch, the men appointed were often incapable of dealing with an emergency. Many of them were not even able-bodied. Several writers of the period have said that a night-watchman was chosen for those qualities that unfitted him to be a night-watchman.

Still, I freely admit that when I see a picture of a frosty night, with the snow sparkling on the roofs and the moon sliding up into the sky, the night-watchman, his red nose above a great muffler, crying: "Twelve o'clock on a frosty night. All's well!" I respond instantly to the romance of a day that is gone.

I am even willing to believe that all night-watchmen were cheery old souls with fine red noses, and were the pride and honour of their various parishes.

Two of them are beyond all censure. They are the last two watchmen left in London who cry the hours at night, and their names are Mr. Wright and Mr. Mongini.

If you go to Ely Place, Holborn Circus, at midnight, you will find the short street of a few houses safe behind locked iron gates. From the porter's lodge in the centre of the barricade will emerge either Mr. Wright or Mr. Mongini.

The watchman will walk slowly down Ely Place and his voice, some-times ably seconded by that of some galli-vanting tom-cat, seems to be the only sound in London.

"Twelve o'clock and a clear frosty night. All's well," he was once supposed to call. But I fear that now he is not so picturesque or meteorological. He just shouts "Past

Twelve," and leaves it at that.

And who, you may ask, ever hears him in Ely Place at night when all the offices are locked and deserted? There are a few resident caretakers, and, at the end of the street, is a convent of Catholic sisters attached to the wonderful little church of Etheldreda's.

"It's a comforting and friendly thing to hear the voice of the night-watchman," said a caretaker. "If any one were ill, I could just open the window and ask him to get a doctor. And, if you can't sleep, or don't feel too well, you listen for his voice and there's something very soothing about it."

At 11 o'clock every night the gates of Ely Place are locked by the watchman. This is the last relic of a peculiarity which once marked out this small street from the rest of London.

Until the middle of the nineteenth century Ely Place was not, technically speaking, in London. There once stood here the ancient palace of the Bishops of Ely, which was immune from civic jurisdiction. It was regarded as a part of the Diocese of Ely by the same sort of fiction which still causes a foreign embassy to be independent of geography. In other words, this little cul-de-sac was a bit of Cambridgeshire set down in London. In the old days the Mitre Tavern, which still exists in a narrow alley, used to receive its licence from Cambridgeshire and was obliged to obey Cambridgeshire times of opening and closing. It is often said in books and newspapers that this tavern is still licensed from Cambridgeshire; but this is not so. But I am assured that should you address a letter to the Mitre Tavern, Ely Place, Cambridgeshire, the postman would deliver it in Holborn without any official asperity.

The queer anomalies of Ely Place began to be straightened out in 1772, when the Bishops of Ely consented to accept 37, Dover Street and hand Ely Place over to the Crown. Then the last vestige of the old palace was pulled down, and the cul-de-sac was rented to an architect, or a builder, who designed its present appearance: a street of discreet Georgian houses originally built for the gentlefolk and now occupied by business firms. The last relic of the Bishop's Palace is the beautiful little chapel of St. Etheldreda at the end of the street, a chapel that, after many vicissitudes, was purchased by the Roman Catholic Fathers of Charity in 1874, and is often claimed to be the only pre-Reformation church in England in which the Mass is still celebrated. This is not so: there is another such church in Northamptonshire.

When the Crown took possession of Ely Place, many of the peculiarities of the street persisted until a special Act of Parliament abolished the territorial privileges and brought the place almost into line with the rest of London.

But to this day the short street is governed by six commissioners, who levy a rate on the tenants for night-watching and street lighting, a matter of 3*d*. or 4*d*. in the pound. The last relic of its former independence is the fact that the police never enter it. It is still in the care of its beadles.

I am told that a thief got in once, when a watchman was looking the other way. A policeman, conscious of the historic peculiarty of Ely Place, requested that the watchman should conduct the intruder outside to the gate, when, knowing that he was on firm London ground, the constable promptly arrested him.

CHAPTER

14

YEOMEN OF THE GUARD

If you could pass through that attractive-looking archway in Friary Court, St. James's Palace, on certain Tuesdays, you would see about thirty middle-aged men in civilian clothes in the act of forming fours. You would notice, perhaps with surprise, that they are all bearded, an unusual sight in these days of the so-called safety-razor.

On every other Tuesday the section, or company, of the

Yeomen of the Guard detailed for duty reports at its head-quarters in Friary Court. There they are told what duties, if any, lie before them in the course of the coming fortnight, and, just to loosen their calf muscles, they do a bit of foot drill, and dismiss.

Their duties, more picturesque, perhaps, than arduous, link them with all manner of strange ghosts of the past. There are few institutions which can boast of a continuous history of four hundred and fifty years.

It is an extraordinary thing that Londoners have not been able in the course of over four and a half centuries to distinguish between the Yeomen of the Guard and the Warders of the Tower of London.

Nearly every year at the opening of Parliament you read in some newspaper, or overhear the remark of an eye-witness, that the "Beefeaters" from the Tower march beside the royal coach. In the first place, the Tower Warders do not recognize the term "Beefeaters"; in the second place, they have nothing to do with the King's coach.

The confusion between the Yeomen and the Warders is due to the almost exact similarity of their uniforms. The only way, in fact, in which you can tell Yeomen of the Guard from Tower Warders, when in full dress, is that the Yeomen of the Guard wear a cross-belt and the Tower Warders do not.

The story of the formation of the Yeomen of the Guard is romantic and interesting. When Richard III had murdered the young Edward V and his brother in the Tower, another claimant to the Throne, Henry Tudor, the only descendant of the old House of Lancaster, was exiled in France, biding his time. He was surrounded by a band of faithful followers. The murder of the princes turned the whole country against Richard, and the time came when Henry landed with a ridiculously meagre force at Milford Haven, marched to meet Richard, slew him on Bosworth Field, and picked the crown out of a thorn bush.

Twenty-three days after the battle of Bosworth a warrant was issued constituting a new corps called "Yeomen of the Guard of our Lord the King," and its first members were the faithful followers who had shared Henry's exile in Brittany and had marched with him through Wales.

There were only thirty-three of them. They were all men whom he could trust with his life, and he needed such men about him. Their first duties were to prevent him from being poisoned or slain in his bed at night, and therefore they were always in close touch with him, guarding the doors, sleeping in the royal bed-chamber, and carrying up the food from the kitchens.

To-day, four hundred and fifty years after, there is a curious echo of the fear that haunted Henry VII in the initials Y.B.G. and Y.B.H., which you will find against the names of certain members of the Yeomen of the Guard. The letters stand for "Yeomen Bed Goers" and "Yeomen Bed Hangers." Although such duties have long since passed away, the ancient titles remain.

There are extraordinarily amusing and detailed instructions in existence telling Yeomen of the Guard how to make the King's bed. First a Yeoman was to take straw and plunge a dagger through it, and, after placing it down, to draw a canvas over it:

Then shall they lay on the bed of down and one of the Yeomen to tumble up and down upon the same for the search thereof, and to beat it and lay it even and smooth . . . then all the said Yeomen to lay hands on the sheet and lay it plain on the bed; then the other fustian or two and such covering as shall best please the king. Then take a pane of ermine and lay it above, then a pane or two of marterns.

Then the Yeoman takes the pillows and beat and raise them well. . . . Then to stick up the angels about the same bed, and an usher to let down the sparver, or curtain, and knit them; and an Esquire for the Body to cast holy water on the same bed.

While the Bed Goers and the Bed Hangers were doing all this,

a groom or page ought to take a torch and fetch a loaf of bread, a pot of ale, and another of wine, and bring it without the traverse, where all they which were at the making of the bed shall go and drink together.

During the reign of Henry VII the uniform of the Yeomen was a simple, braided tunic embroidered with a Tudor rose. Henry VIII, however, in his desire to appear grander than any other monarch, overloaded his attendants with "spangles gilt and white, letter wreaths, harts and roses of fine gold and goldsmith's embroidery" until one wonders how they were ever able to sit down.

He bought them horse-cloths of gold at £5 a yard, probably when he was setting off for that extravagant meeting with the King of France, known as the Field of the Cloth of Gold, where even the sand was powdered with gold-dust.

Meanwhile the Tower Warders, who in very ancient times had guarded the king when he stayed in the Tower, began to feel that this new bodyguard might in time deprive them of their privileges.

As a corps, these warders are undoubtedly the oldest band of men still performing their original duties, for the corps is obviously as old as the Tower. Their dissatisfaction with what seemed to them a new-fangled bodyguard of Yeomen found expression in 1551 when the Duke of Somerset was a prisoner in the Tower.

They formed a deputation and begged him on his release to use his influence to restore to them their ancient dress and privileges; and he did not forget his promise.

The result was that the Tower Warders were given the same uniform as the Yeomen of the Guard, with the exception of the cross-belt. In the Tower regulations they are set down as "Honorary" members of the Bodyguard of the Yeomen of the Guard.

"Beefeater" is a name they do not like. No one knows quite what it means. (Perhaps the best explanation is that it means an eater of beef.) Neither the Tower Warders nor the Yeomen of the Guard were ever in charge of the royal refreshment room, so that the popular explanation that "Beefeater" is a corruption of "buffetier" is probably quite erroneous.

Both corps are recruited from non-commissioned officers of the army. The strength of the Yeomen of the Guard is about a hundred. They are divided into sections which take duty in rotation. They live in their own homes and are billeted in St. James's Palace only when on night duty. They must be sergeants with long service medals and other decorations, and they receive about £40 a year in addition to their pensions.

One of their busiest associates is the wardrobe master, whose duty it is to keep the hundred gay and gold-braided uniforms in good condition, to see that the moth does not get into the red stockings, or dust into the Tudor rosettes.

Now and again the duties of Tower Warders and the Yeomen of the Guard almost coincide. On the eve of the opening of Parliament the Yeomen Warder of the Tower takes the Crown (generally in a taxi-cab) to the Houses of Parliament: but it is the Yeomen of the Guard who, on the following morning, guard the Crown as they march beside the king's coach.

Perhaps the most interesting parade of the Yeomen of

the Guard is their annual search for Guy Fawkes in the vaults of the Houses of Parliament. Although the vaults are now well illuminated by electricity, they go down carrying lanterns with lit candles in them.

The search always concludes with cake and wine. This is a relic of the old, old days before the present Houses of Parliament were built, when in 1773, old John Bellamy, a wine merchant, was appointed Deputy Caterer to the House of Commons. His port and his pork pies were famous. "I think I could eat one of Bellamy's pork pies," were the last words uttered on his death-bed by the great Pitt.

Old Bellamy used part of the vaults as a wine-cellar, and every time the Yeomen of the Guard came down on their annual search for traitors an old joke would be worked off on him.

"Those barrels look as though they might hold a body!" a Yeoman would say.

"And so they do, my boy!" Bellamy would reply. "All my tipple down here is full-bodied; taste and try!"

I imagine that the modern cake and wine is probably a pale ghost of old John Bellamy's hospitality.

CHAPTER
15

ROYAL WAXWORKS

If you wish to see the last relic of the pageantry with which a nobleman was buried in mediæval England, you must go down to Whitechapel.

Any insurance agent that canvasses the poor streets of East London will tell you how many hundreds of thousands of pounds are tied up in funeral money, for there is no disgrace so deep as that of being buried by the parish. Therefore countless poor people stint themselves in their last years to save the 3*d*. or 6*d*. a week which will pay for nodding plumes on black horses, and a cold collation afterwards with wine and beer.

This is a tradition that goes back to the richest days of our history. It might have been thought that when this country became Protestant, and the theory of Purgatory, with its belief in the efficacy of prayers for the dead, was abandoned, funeral ceremonies would have become more simple. But this was not so. The Requiem Mass was abolished, but the candles, the pall, the catafalque, the black cloth and the funeral bake-meats remained.

It may seem strange that, although a dead duke may be hurried almost furtively through the streets in a motor-hearse, those who can least afford the ancient pomp of death slave and scrape to provide the pale semblance of a ducal funeral.

Those unconscious traditionalists who spend their last farthing on a funeral have many a noble precedent. So elaborate and expensive were funerals in the old days that ancient families ruined themselves in paying last honours to their dead. Charles II ordered that his friend, the Duke of Rothes, should be buried like a royal personage, and his unfortunate family, believing that the King would pay, mortgaged their estates to raise the necessary money. But Charles forgot to do so. When the body of that impoverished paragon, Sir Philip Sidney, was brought home from the Low

Countries, it lay unburied for three months because no one could be found to advance the great sum necessary for an adequate funeral.

A Queen of England lay dead in Somerset House from the end of March until May 13th because there was no money to pay for the elaborate funeral that had been decreed for her. This was Anne of Denmark, consort of James I. Eventually her body was taken to Westminster in a decorated hearse, surmounted by her image made in life-like wax, and drawn by six jet-black horses, plumed and draped in sable.

During the Republic under Cromwell, when all kinds of ceremonies lapsed, the pomp of funerals was kept up, presumably as a reaction against the prevailing gloom. While Puritans went round knocking off the beautifully carved heads on the cathedrals because they were "idols," no one, strangely enough, considered idolatrous the wax effigies carried in funeral processions.

Those effigies, during the Commonwealth, were wonderfully made and coloured. Their joints were flexible so that they could be seated in a coach during the funeral procession and afford a life-like image of the departed.

One of the most pompous funerals of that time was the burial of Robert Devereux, Earl of Essex, the Parliamentary commander-in-chief. It took the best part of a day for his procession to pass from the Strand to Westminster, and the crowds who lined the route gazed with pleasure at a life-like figure of the dead Earl, sitting up in an open chariot drawn by six horses whose velvet palls swept the ground.

As recently as two hundred years ago middle-class people spent vast sums with the undertakers. A note of ghoulish enjoyment seems to have crept into the English funeral of the eighteenth century. The invitation cards sent out by relatives are enough to make one's blood run cold.

I have one of the reign of Queen Anne before me at the moment. Shaped like a tombstone, it shows on the top Father Time leaning carelessly on a skull, balanced on the other side by the figure of Death with a spear in his claws. Beneath this is the rather pointless advice, "Remember to die."

The invitation is flanked by pictures of hour-glasses, skeletons, crossed leg-bones, shovels, pick-axes and a shroud. In the centre of this ghastly border are the words:

Sir, you are invited to Accompany the Corps of Mr. Thomas Newborough from his late Dwelling-house in St. Paul's Churchyard, to the Burial-place of St. Gregory's on Wednesday, the 29th instant, at Five of the Clock in the afternoon.

At this period the old custom was still observed of draping houses inside and outside with lengths of black cloth. This is still done in France and other Continental countries.

Numerous advertisements of undertakers in the eighteenth century prove how much importance was paid by our ancestors to the outward show of death, and also how

keen was the competition among members of the under-
taking trade. Here is a typical advertisement:

For the good of the Publick, I, Edward Evans, at the Four Coffins in the Strand, over against Somerset House, furnish all Neces-
saries for all sorts of Funerals both great and small. And all sorts
of set Mourning, both Black and Gray, and all other furniture
suitable to it, fit for any person of Quality. Which I promise to
perform 2s. in the Pound cheaper than any of the Undertakers in
Town, or elsewhere.

That anyone could trade under the sign of the Four
Coffins in the Strand seems to me to indicate the difference
between an age of stark realism and an age, like our own,
full of all manner of hypocritical evasion. Among the things
which astonish a visitor to the United States are the sentimental advertisements of the "mortician"; for so the un-
dertaker is called on the other side of the Atlantic. The
atmosphere of gin-sodden grief which he contrives to cast
around his "parlour" is, to my mind, either nauseating or
amusing. He frequently refers in print to the "dear ones"
whom it is his privilege to "put to rest," with more affection
than seems decent in a stranger. I much prefer the blunt
honesty of Edward Evans and his Four Coffins. Nevertheless
the American "mortician" is the only person who has devel-
oped a "new angle" on the practical issues of death, and it
is interesting to note that while the Old World, harking
back to princely processions, loved lavish display and the

trappings of state, the New World stresses the quiet homely atmosphere of a well-bred funeral.

If, therefore, you wish to see some real ghosts of London go to Westminster Abbey and look at the eleven wax-work figures which are still exhibited to the curious in the upper floor of Abbot Islip's Chapel.

Many of them are the actual effigies carried in those State funerals that were so dear to the hearts of the London crowd centuries ago. The best figure is that of Charles II. The life-like figure of Queen Elizabeth was remade in 1760 from an earlier model. The figures of William III, Mary and Queen Anne are interesting. A few years ago the effigy of the young Duke of Buckingham, after having been cleaned and restored by the Victoria and Albert Museum, was added to the royal waxworks. This figure is exactly as it was when carried through the London streets on January 31st, 1736.

The face, like that of many of the others, is evidently a death mask. The body is made of canvas stuffed with straw. The young man, who died of consumption at the age of nineteen, wears the red velvet mantle of a duke, red velvet breeches and, beneath the mantle, a magnificent rose-coloured silk coat.

His shoes are of white leather with red heels. The curled wig is made of human hair, and is still heavily powdered with orris-root. The maker's name can be read on a label inside the wig, "Francis Caraffa, Peruke Maker, next door to the Rummer Tavern in Gerrard St., St. Anne's, Soho,"

Strange as it may seem, there is a definite link between our waxen monarchs and those people in humble places who spend far more than they can afford on the pageantry of death. Every time a Cockney funeral goes past, with plumes nodding from the hearse and ostrich feathers tossing on the harness, one sees the last ghost of those dismal processions in torchlight which brought the startled villagers of England from their beds at night, and told them that a great man had been gathered to his rest.

CHAPTER
16

BELLS OF ST. PAUL'S

The City of London expires promptly every night. London's most crowded mile then becomes the most desolate. Secretaries and typists, who bring so much charm and grace to what would otherwise be an undignified scramble for gain, put on their hats and, contrary to the traditions of Hollywood, go home.

Clerks who slave, with or without the dreams that alone

redeem slavery, grasp their umbrellas and go their ways. Sinful "bulls" and unspeakable "bears" turn with a greedy grunt from the tape machines and slink, one imagines, towards the West.

The moment comes when Mr. Montagu Norman leaves the Bank of England, perhaps in disguise, possible by a back door; and the old Square Mile, wrapped in a spurious innocence, crouches in the shadow of the centuries. What a ghostly place it is at night! The omnibuses lift themselves heavily and wearily up Ludgate Hill like timid explorers, reluctant to invade the desert that leads to Liverpool Street. Roads which by day are so crowded with men, so loud with the thunder of wheels, fall into silence and become so safe that the most leisurely cat in London has time to wash his face on a walk from the Mansion House to the Bank.

It is at such a moment that the twelve great bells of St. Paul's Cathedral sometimes decide to crash into music. It begins with a startling "zoom" from the treble bell, followed instantly by a gigantic somersault of bells, so loud, so triumphant, so terrifying in that still hour that even Justice must tremble on top of the Old Bailey, and many a fat pigeon must have died of heart failure in the darkness of the bell-tower. The peals go rocketing over silent London. They go cascading up Fleet Street towards the Strand. They play hide and seek in Ave Maria Lane, and they chase each other up and down Paternoster Row.

A stranger might well wonder what obscure occasion

was causing this great church to rejoice in the darkness as the bell music becomes wilder and more intricate. The belfry rocks with joy.

It seems to be greeting an invisible wedding party that should be winding its way up Ludgate Hill. The peals go gambolling through the old lanes of London as if begging the ghosts of the merchants of Chepe to come forth from their homes and toss their caps in the air in rejoicing for every victory won by English arms from Crécy to the Armada.

That, at least, is how I feel about it when, once a fortnight, the Ancient Society of College Youths holds a bell practice in St. Paul's.

I was invited the other night by a College youth (who has just celebrated his silver wedding) to attend a bell practice of the Society. Entering St. Paul's by a little side door in the churchyard, we mounted a spiral stair, and, after a long climb, reached a room in the bell-tower from whose ceiling fell twelve ropes.

A number of College Youths in their shirt-sleeves stood about talking the queer jargon of their ancient craft: Stedman Cinques, peals of Treble Bob Maximus, Grandsire Triples; and all the rest of it, terms known only to bell-ringers.

I was not sufficiently innocent to expect all College Youths to be rosy-faced lads, but I was not prepared for many of them to be rosy-faced old men with white beards. One of the Youths told me that he was over seventy, and that he had known a man who had spoken to another man who had taken part in a ring of Stedman Caters in 1755.

"Bell-ringers live to a great age," I was told. "Bell-ringing hardens the stomach muscles. It prevents that flabbiness that causes all kinds of internal troubles after the age of forty."

I noticed three women, ready in skirts and jumpers, to ring the bells.

"Are there also College Maidens?" I asked.

"Oh no," I was told. "These ladies are visiting bell-ringers and have been invited to take part in the practice. It is, of course, a great honour to ring the bells of St. Paul's."

The ringers moved to the ropes. They grasped them. There was a moment of suspense. Someone said "Treble going!"; and the next second the bells of St. Paul's crashed out over London.

The ancient Society of College Youths began its bell-ringing when Charles I was king; and its members have been ringing the bells of London ever since. The walls of the bell-tower are decorated with the record of their historic achievements, such as the four-hour long peal of Stedman Cinques of 5,014 changes, which they rang on November 23rd, 1918, to celebrate the end of the War.

The College from which they derive their historic

youthfulness was the College of the Holy Ghost and Hospital of God's House, founded by Dick Whittington in Upper Thames Street in 1422. This building was destroyed in the Great Fire, but the ghost of it haunts London in the title of this Society.

No one knows how many members are in existence. Once a member, always a member. If you can satisfy the Master and members of the College Youths that you can ring a bell in 1,260 changes of some standard method, you may be nominated, proposed and seconded, and elected.

Having paid a fee of 7s. 6d., you will be endowed with life-long youth, for your membership terminates only with life itself. There must be many hundreds of, so to speak, lost College Youths all over the country, but the real Society is composed of active, ringing members, who ring the bells of St. Paul's every Sunday, practise there every fortnight, and are ready at any moment of national importance to furnish a "band" of ringers for Westminster Abbey, or any other belfry that requires expert attention.

The Society is a thriving ghost of old London. Its activities go back to the time when London was an overgrown country town, and when the church bells really did pull citizens from their beds on Sunday mornings and send them hurrying to church.

I learnt a number of things as the bells of St. Paul's went mad overhead. I learnt, first of all, that bell-ringing is an intricate and difficult art, whose finer points date from 1668, when Fabian Stedman, who was a Cambridge printer, devised the intricate method of scientific change-ringing that elevates bell-ringing into the region of the mathematical arts.

A bell can be chimed or rung. When you chime a bell, it is hanging mouth down and you move the clapper so that it strikes the side of the bell. When you ring a bell—as the bells of St. Paul's are rung every Sunday—the bell is first "set," or gradually worked up until its mouth points upward, and is then "pulled off," making at each note almost a complete circle.

So that when you hear the bells of St. Paul's, or any other great church, ringing changes, you can imagine the bells turning over this way and then that way, but never re-maining still.

Then I learnt that a group of ringers is called a "band," that one of the ringers is called the "conductor," and that the changes that are rung are written by a composer. When bells are rung in the same order from the treble to the heaviest bell—the tenor—they are said to be ringing in "rounds," but when this order is varied they are ringing "changes."

The number of possible changes is staggering. To find out how many changes you can get from a given number of bells, you must multiply them together. Thus 3 bells give 6 changes or variations of order, 4 bells give 24, 5 bells give 120, 6 bells give 720, 7 bells give 5,040; and so on.

Those of us who know nothing about bells use the word "peal" very loosely. Bell-ringers do not recognize a peal of six bells until all the changes possible for six bells (720) have been repeated continuously seven times. In other words, 5,040 bell notes must be made before six bells have, in the ears of an expert, "pealed."

But I shall get into deep water if I try to explain this without a blackboard! You must take it from me that a bell-ringer requires the mind of a senior wrangler, the eye of a hawk, the ear of a musician, and the biceps of a healthy human being.

"Band" after "band" of ringers had succeeded to the ropes, and the bells of St. Paul's had played "rounds" and "changes."

I was lost in admiration for the various conductors who, keeping the infinite variations in their minds, shouted hoarse and inarticulate commands to their fellow ringers, who, by the way, rang as much from "rope-sense" as anything else; that is, the automatic knowledge of the ropes to be pulled before and after one's own rope.

Once, and once only, some one managed to pull a fraction too soon, or too late, with the result that two bells sounded almost at once, and the conductor roared out a command. My sympathies were all with the unfortunate ringer.

Mr. Hamburg may make a little slip on the piano and

nobody may notice it. Kreisler may be allowed some margin of error. But you cannot possibly pretend that you were not really ringing the tenor bell of St. Paul's Cathedral!

Eventually the College Youths, panting slightly, resumed their jackets:

"Will you come with us to the 'Coffee Pot' in Warwick Lane?" I was asked. "We hold our fortnightly meeting there, and rarely admit strangers and non-ringers."

CHAPTER
17

AT THE "COFFEE POT"

We came down from the bell-tower and saw the lamp-light throwing shadows among the trees in St. Paul's churchyard. Ludgate Hill was hushed and empty in the darkness. My head throbbed with the vibration of the bells that had for the last hour clashed out over the dark city.

A young man met us, leaning against a bicycle. He was the son of a College Youth. He made some comment on the bells, and told us that he had cycled from his home in Whitechapel to listen to them. I forgot how many times he had cycled round St. Paul's during the practice.

His presence gave me the clue to something I had been seeking all that evening. There he was with his bicycle, rather like a village youth cycling round the village church.

I thought that in the historic functions of ancient societies like the College Youths, the bewildering city of London shrinks and dwindles to the size of a village. Every time such old societies meet, London becomes small enough to love.

It is easy to forget in restaurants, hotels, cinemas, and in Shaftesbury Avenue on a Saturday afternoon, where you scarcely see one English face, that this apparently incoherent and international city loses its vast impersonality whenever ancient societies meet to ring church bells, to administer old charities, or to eat together as their members have done for centuries. To such people, who alone deserve the name of Londoners, the city is not merely a bewildering money-bag or a vulgar amusement park; it is still an overgrown country town in which a man can feel at home.

The "Coffee Pot" stands at a corner of Warwick Lane, near Amen Corner and Paternoster Row—names which are ghosts of pre-Reformation London. In an upper room of the tavern the Ancient Society transacts its business every fortnight.

I was challenged at the door by a steward who, noting a new face, pounced on me with the question: "Are you a member?" A College Youth came to my rescue, and I was admitted to a room in which about fifty bell-ringers sat facing a table and a row of chairs.

"The second rule of the Society," explained my friend, "states that no stranger may be present at our meetings without the consent of the Master. It is usual for a member introducing a stranger to stand up and ask permission for his friend to remain, but we have waived the rule to-night."

I was given a seat near the Master, who solemnly invested himself with his badge of office, a blue ribbon from which hung a silver medal. Officers of the society had meanwhile placed on the table the interesting regalia of the society. There was an elaborate silver mace whose head was a bell, there were various silver cups, the Master's hammer, in the form of a bell, and two brass candlesticks which were used by the Duke of Wellington throughout the Peninsular campaign. Before the Ancient Society of College Youths holds its meetings, the candles in these sticks are always lighted, and when they are snuffed it is a sign that all business is over.

The Duke of Wellington, I gathered, had no connexion with the society, and was not apparently interested in bell-ringing. The candlesticks were the gift of a friend of the society many years ago.

The business transacted by the bell-ringers was of a practical and technical character. While the candles in the Iron Duke's candlesticks guttered every time a steward opened a door, the secretary read out the minutes of the last meeting, and the Master submitted various resolutions, all connected with the belfry.

The College Youth sitting next to me was a grizzled old man who told me that he was a sexton. On the other side sat a College Youth of over seventy, who, although he does not often grasp a rope these days, enjoys attending, in a spirit of critical enjoyment, bell practices and the subsequent meetings.

I was handed a large book which contained the names of all College Youths from the year 1637, the date of the society's foundation, to the year 1871.

If this society is typical of bell-ringers all over the country, this pastime must indeed be a happy one. There were men of every type, age, trade and profession. It was a democracy of tintinnabulation.

Unlike many other ancient organizations, the College Youths have no use for honorary members. It is impossible to buy your way into the ancient company: you must be prepared to take off your coat in a belfry and prove to the Master and his associates that you can ring at least 1,260 changes.

At last the moment came when a new College Youth, who had passed this drastic test, was admitted to the fellowship. He had been carefully excluded from the proceedings, but now the door was flung open and a steward called him in. Tankards and glasses were put down, for bell-ringers do not conduct their business sadly, and faces were turned to the door.

In walked a middle-aged man.

He shook hands with the Master, who welcomed him into the ranks of the College Youths, expressing the hope that he would do nothing to disgrace the ancient and honourable fellowship of bell-ringers, whose motto is, "Let us live in Unity."

Suddenly the meeting was closed, the candles were snuffed, the regalia were packed away in baize-lined boxes, and the Master said:

"Now, let's have a touch on the hand-bells!"

While he, with several other College Youths, sat round in a circle, each man grasping two hand-bells, the stewards entered bearing the final trays of beer.

Pipes were lit, and we settled down to enjoy a remarkable performance. The hand-bells, that I had heard previously only on the stage, had generally been loud and unpleasant, but these bells were muffled and sent out a sweet sound, rather like the sound of church bells heard far off over meadows.

They rang in intricate unity for perhaps half an hour. I sat there thinking how worthily the College Youths carry on their trust. If there were ghosts of other College

Youths in Warwick Lane that night—and who knows what ghosts the bells of St. Paul's stir from the shadows—I am sure that they must have cocked appreciative ears towards the upper room of the "Coffee Pot."

It is in such simple happy gatherings that London turns her back on vulgarity and keeps faith with her past.

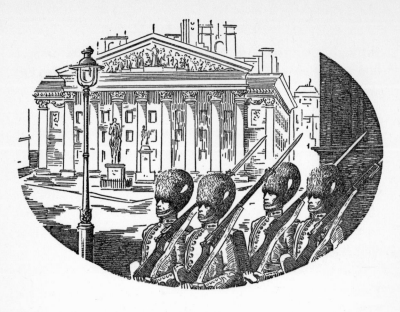

CHAPTER

18

BANK GUARD

Through the crowded streets of the City of London, and
at the busiest hour of the evening, a company of about
twenty-four soldiers marches to the Bank of England.

They wear the black bearskins of the Guards and they
carry, as only privileged troops may do, fixed bayonets
past the Mansion House. On those days when the Scots or
the Irish Guards are performing guard duties, they come

through the maze of omnibuses, taxicabs, and urgent homeward crowds, led by a piper whose high notes skirl above the noise of wheels and changing gears.

I am not concerned, as politicians may be, whether the great fortress of Finance should be guarded or whether it should be left to the untender mercies of the night. I am interested only in this custom as a ghost of London: one of those strange things that happen every day and, although part and parcel of our lives, is, by virtue of its history, exceptional and interesting and rooted in something that happened long ago.

The correct term for the Bank Guard is the Bank Piquet. Few people know very much about it beyond the fact that it was established years ago, during a riot. There is also a legend that the officer in charge receives a brand-new sovereign (some say a bottle of wine) at the expense of the Directors of the Bank.

With a certain amount of pains, I have unearthed the story of the Bank Piquet from the archives of the War Office.

In June, 1780, a crack-brained agitator, Lord George Gordon, headed a mob of many thousands of people to protest against the removal of Catholic disabilities. Gordon, after a rather eccentric career, had accepted the presidency of the Protestant Association, an organization pledged to secure the repeal of the Catholic Relief Act of 1778.

The mob that gathered round him, when he took the monster petition to Parliament, was infinitely more interested in plunder than Protestantism, and, getting out of hand, began to burn down the houses of Catholics. Having tasted blood, they then decided to taste alcohol, and sacked several breweries.

Things became dangerous. London endured a reign of terror for days. Enormous mobs paraded the streets, fighting drunk, armed with every kind of weapon, smashing, plundering and burning. They burned down Newgate and several other prisons, and, reinforced by two thousand criminals, continued to riot day and night. The time came when they decided to attack the Bank of England. The Lord Mayor of London appealed to the Government for horse and foot guards, and, in response, five hundred and thirty-four men were sent, also a band of citizen volunteers which included John Wilkes.

The attack on the Bank began after eleven at night. It was led by a brewer's drayman hung about with chains from Newgate Prison, mounted on a shire horse. The troops fired twice, killing two men, and the main body of rioters drew off.

In the early hours of the morning a second attack was made from Cheapside. This also was beaten off with a casualty list of eight killed and many wounded. Firm action in other parts of London finally ended the Gordon Riots.

Gordon himself, although sent to the Tower, was acquitted of high treason. He continued his eccentric career, adopted Judaism, and died insane in Newgate Prison where, for the three years before his death, he gave dinner-parties and dances and amused himself by playing the bagpipes; he also grew a long beard and observed the Passover.

The Gordon Riots therefore necessitated the Bank Piquet, and troops have been on duty ever since, except during Parliamentary elections of the eighteenth century when, under an ancient Act, all troops quartered in the City had to be moved to a distance of two miles beyond the boundaries. During such periods a volunteer band of clerks and watchmen patrolled the Bank at night.

The Guard, however, was not popular with the City authorities, who viewed its nightly march as a serious infringement of ancient City privileges. More than one attempt was made by magistrates to obstruct the passage of the Guard, and an offer was made to provide a guard from members of the Honourable Artillery Company.

The bad feeling between the City and the Piquet came to a head in 1790, when a magistrate decided to oppose the nightly "invasion." This champion of City privilege was the Lord Mayor-elect (Alderman Picket, appropriately enough), who obstructed the Bank Guard, meeting it on Ludgate Hill and attempting to turn it back; but he was told officially that, if the guards were not permitted to carry out their duties in peace, the Bank would be removed to Somerset House.

Soldiers were always provided with blankets, bread, cheese and beer at the expense of the Directors of the Bank. The officer was allowed dinner, which was brought in to him from a neighbouring tavern.

In 1788 Bank barracks were built for the guard, and in 1792, as the result of much grousing about the weight of cheese and the quality of the beer supplied, the Bank decided to give the allowance in money; 1s. 6d. for each sergeant and 10d. for each man.

The officer, in addition to his dinner, was allowed to ask two friends to dine with him, in which event he was entitled to three bottles of wine. On Sunday, April 14, 1793, the only fight since the Gordon Riots took place when the two guests invited by the officer enjoyed themselves so much that they refused to go home. They resisted every suggestion of departure, and fought their host rather than leave the scene of so much happiness to themselves.

In the words of a report on this incident, they "used indecent and abusive language and slept all night at the Bank, after breaking bottles and glasses and fighting together with the officer in the Bank yard."

In spite of this incident the generous wine allowance was continued, and the officer was still allowed to while away the weary hours by inviting two friends to dinner.

Throughout the Napoleonic Wars the Bank Piquet continued to function, and a popular move was the increase of the sergeants' allowance to 2s. a night and the privates' to 1s.

In 1821 the Directors established a wine-cellar at the Bank, and the officer on duty therefore drew his bottle of port or sherry, "or a pint of each sort if he preferred it," from the Bank vaults, although his dinner came in as usual from the King's Head Tavern.

Tremendous preparations for trouble were made at the Bank during the Reform Riots of 1830, and in 1848, when the Chartists prepared their monster petition, the Bank was sand-bagged, loop-holed and fortified.

When rebuilding operations were started on the Bank of England in 1924, the rusted and obsolete "machinery of defence" was discovered and removed from the roof. It had remained there for seventy-two years.

To-night the Bank Piquet will file into the hall of the Bank at a quarter past six if it is fine, and earlier if it is wet.

The men tramp in single file, and with a loud ring of service boots, across the classic entrance hall with its pillars of black marble.

They have been making this entry for a hundred and fifty-five years. Nothing has ever happened during that time except, as I have said, a little exuberance on the part of the subaltern's guests, and once or twice the mysterious disappearance of the subaltern himself.

But in these days, when drink is fortunately no longer

a social accomplishment, the years provide the spectacle of a long line of exemplary subalterns. As a reward for good conduct, perhaps, the Directors of the Bank have, during the present reconstructions, provided the officer with a pleasing suite of rooms: a bedroom, a bathroom, and a sitting-room.

In this sitting-room he is still, by ancient custom, permitted to entertain a male guest, who must leave the Bank by 11 o'clock; but his wine and his dinner come nowadays from a kitchen which I believe is excellent, and one which in the day-time ministers to certain members of the Bank staff.

THE BANK PIQUET

CHAPTER
19

NAILS AS RENT

One of the strangest ceremonies I have ever seen in a law court is the payment of nails and horse-shoes that the City of London makes to the Crown every year. This quit-rent is one of the last surviving examples of the feudal system of land tenure.

Writers frequently state that, with the exception of the Coronation, this ceremony is the oldest in the country, but they forget a much older one: the annual open-air assembly of the House of Keys on Tynwald Hill in the Isle of Man. That is the last example of an open-air folk-moot in Europe and goes back to Viking days.

However, the quit-rent ceremony, as a ghost of Norman London, is old enough to make us gasp with astonishment when it is solemnly carried out every year by a number of serious-looking men in brindle wigs. The payment is made as rent for a portion of land to the north of Chancery Lane. The story behind this land takes us back in imagination to the London of 1235 when the Knights Templars had their quarters just outside the City boundary on the ground still called the Temple. Formed during the First Crusade to fight for the holy places, those "Poor Knights of Christ and of the Temple of Solomon" rapidly amassed wealth and power in all European countries.

Their Temple in London, with its beautiful little Round Church, which still exists, included a great monastery, cloisters and meadows near the river, where their war horses were trained. The Strand, which is, of course, the strand, or shore, of the Thames, was at that time—the reign of Henry III—thinly dotted with houses leading from Ludgate towards the village of Charing, and more or less following the line of the present Strand. Opposite the Temple the road was bordered by meadows, where Chancery Lane and the Law Courts stand to-day.

A memory of the meadowlands is still preserved in the

name of Lincoln's Inn Fields, which, at the time I am writing about, were country fields and pasture land lying at the back of the Strand and joining up with the garden of the monks of Westminster, known as Convent Garden. This abbey property was said to cover an area of seven acres, one of them a long acre strip of land bordered by elm trees. Its memory is perpetuated by the street name of Long Acre.

The Knights Templars were in the habit of using the meadows opposite their property as a tournament ground. It must have been more suitable for such a purpose than the sloping river bank on which their buildings were constructed.

In this place the sunburnt knights re-enacted the mighty feats of arms performed in the Holy Land, and presumably kept themselves in training for the next crusade.

On one occasion in the year 1235, legend relates that a Templar named Walter le Brun, who was taking part in a tournament, needed a smith to shoe the fore-feet of his charger. He asked the help of a man who, in order to be ready to mend broken armour and harness, had established a portable forge in a corner of the ground. One imagines that this smith probably attended the place only on tournament days.

His services to Walter le Brun were so highly appreciated that he was given permission to build a permanent forge in the south-east corner of Ficket's Croft, as the meadow was called, which some people believe lay somewhere at the Fleet Street end of the present Chancery Lane. There is another theory that the land lay nearer the Thames. The rent demanded of him (whether to the Crown or the Knights Templars, I cannot say) was a quit-rent of six horse-shoes, and the nails to go with them.

How and when the piece of land on which the smith used to shoe the crusaders' horses came into the possession of the City of London no one can say.

When the Order of the Templars was abolished by the Pope in 1312, the Crown took possession of the Temple, and it was not until 1608, in the time of James I, that this land passed from the possession of the Crown to the Benchers of the Inner and the Middle Temple. It has been suggested that the records linking the City with the forge in Ficket's Croft were destroyed when Wat Tyler and his men made a bonfire of so many ancient documents.

However, every year the Crown demands from the City the ancient quit-rent that the smith paid for his land seven hundred years ago.

The King's Remembrancer presides over the ceremony in his full-bottomed wig and gown. Two warrants, in language even more archaic and difficult to understand than that habitually used by lawyers, are read out to the court, and the tenants are ordered to "come forth and do your service."

The City Solicitor then steps forward and carefully

counts out six horse-shoes and the nails to go with them.
The horse-shoes are of an enormous size and have been in
the possession of the City for something like five hundred
years. They are all fore-shoes of knights' chargers, and it
is interesting to note that they are formed as weapons for
the horses' feet. War horses of the Middle Ages were carefully schooled in warlike deportment, and were trained to
help their riders, when in close contact with the enemy,
by rising on their haunches and aiming blows with their
fore-feet; an attitude seen in battle pictures as late as the
time of Marlborough.

After the City Solicitor has performed the formality of
counting the nails and the horse-shoes, he puts them in his
bag and takes them back with him to Guildhall!

To those of practical mind, the strangest thing about
the ceremony is the fact that neither Crown nor City has
the slightest idea where the land is to be found for which
the quit-rent is offered! Therefore, the ceremony has no
meaning, and is kept up from year to year purely from
sentimental motives.

How charming! How delightful to observe the Crown
and the City meeting once a year to count their horse-shoes
like a couple of middle-aged lovers who fondly show one
another the keepsakes of youth!

CHAPTER

20

BEATING THE BOUNDS

Every three years, on Ascension Day, or during Rogation Week, the Yeoman Gaoler of the Tower walks out into the streets of London with the axe over his shoulder.

Behind, two by two, march the Warders of the Tower in their full-dress uniform: scarlet tunics, breeches, red stockings, Tudor bonnets, and shoes with tricoloured rosettes on the toes. Each man carries a halberd.

The carters, who are held up to allow this strange procession to pass, become extremely witty and historical at the expense of the Warders, sometimes leaning from high perches to shout questions about Henry VIII and Anne Boleyn.

Behind the Warders walk all the resident children in the Tower of London; and there are a surprising number of them in the married quarters. They are given a school holiday on this popular day, and they walk, holding peeled willow wands, which are handed out to each boy and girl before the procession is formed. This ceremony is the ancient Beating the Bounds of the Tower Liberties, and it is the ghost of an England that existed long before the Tower of London. The custom of beating the bounds is mentioned in the laws of Alfred the Great and Athelstan.

Led by the Chief Yeoman Warder carrying the Tower Mace, the procession marches up to Tower Hill. It halts before a warehouse wall, on which one of the boundary marks is visible.

"Now whip it, boys, whip it!" orders the Chief Warder; and a number of boys advance on the stone and set about it with their willow switches.

Another boundary stone is opposite the Mint. The same process is repeated. The line of march then goes down to the edge of the Thames, below Tower Bridge, where a stone just above tide level is soundly thrashed. There are thirty-one boundary marks of the Tower Liberty still in existence, and one of the last is concealed in a small outhouse under Tower Bridge.

The procession then returns to the Tower of London, whose boundaries may now be considered safe for another three years.

At the same time of year the Parish of St. Clement Danes in the Strand sometimes decides to beat its boundaries. This church possesses an ancient hammer engraved with the date 1573. It was used in Tudor times to keep order at the feast which followed the ceremony.

In the old days there were nearly a hundred boundary marks in this parish, but I believe that only about twenty of them can be found to-day. This shows how hard it is for a modern parish to find its mediæval limits, because the rebuilding of London has caused new roads to be driven over parish frontiers, and many a house on which the ancient marks were visible was swept out of existence centuries ago.

The ceremony begins in the vaults of Child's Bank in Fleet Street, and then passes through the Outer Temple to Essex Court and New Court and down to the fine lawn of the Middle Temple.

The next stage of the journey takes the beaters out on to the Thames. They step into rowing-boats and make for a point in the middle of the river, returning to Shell Mex House, the site of the old Hotel Cecil, visiting the

BEATING THE BOUNDS, TOWER OF LONDON

stage of the Lyceum Theatre, which is half in and half out of the parish, King's College, Strand Lane, Lincoln's Inn, New Square, and then back to the church of St. Clement Danes in the centre of the Strand.

The beating of the marks is performed by the choir boys of the church, and I believe that, now and then, one of them is "bumped"; that is to say, the lad is turned upside down and bumped two or three times on the site of the boundary.

What is the origin of this custom? Some antiquaries have traced it back to Roman times, and to celebrations in honour of Terminus, the Roman god of boundaries. We can say with certainty that the custom has existed in this country for over a thousand years.

Its object was obviously to impress on the minds of the youngest persons in a parish the limitations of the parish, so that, in an age when maps were not common, those children, when they grew up, would all be able to testify to the ancient boundary stones.

When Beating the Bounds was a really serious affair and carried out with religious observance by every parish in the land, the children were often soundly beaten at the various marks, the better to impress these limitations on their minds.

It is clear that good hidings were saved up for this occasion. A writer who lived in the late eighteenth century says that where Oxford Street and Tottenham Court Road now meet, there used to be a large circular boundary-stone let into the pavement.

"When," he says, "the charity boys of St. Giles's parish walk the boundaries, those who have deserved flogging are whipped at this stone, in order that, when they grow up, they may remember the place and be competent to give evidence should any dispute arise with the neighbouring parishes."

CHAPTER

21

"REMEMBER THE GROTTER"

Round about July 25—but the date is capable of wide variation—you may have noticed that London children gather a few flowers and ferns and, with the aid of a candle, a bit of tinsel and a few oyster shells, compose a little show on the pavement. They come up to you and say: "Remember the grotto," although in many districts the pronunciation is "grotter."

Sometimes a child will run beside you singing out a rhyme, or several children will chant it together. If you can persuade them to repeat it slowly, this is what you will hear:

Please to remember the grotter,
It's only once a year,
Father's gone to sea and mother's gone to fetch him back,
So please remember me.
'A'penny won't hurt yer;
Tuppence won't put yer in the work'us.

I daresay you may have wondered why they do this, and why the passer-by should be expected to contribute to what is, when all is said and done, a poor little side-show.

Those children have no idea why they build the "grottoes." They do so because other children have done so, and because it is well known that now and then a kindly stranger will bestow a penny on the "grotto." This in itself is enough to keep alive the custom, for even in these days a penny will buy a bag of sweets.

Of all the strange ghosts which haunt the streets of London the July grottoes on the pavement are among the most surprising: they are an unconscious survival of the great emotion which, in the Middle Ages, sent hundreds and thousands of Catholic pilgrims from this country to the shrine of St. James, the son of Zebedee, in the great Cathedral of Santiago, in the North-West of Spain.

Centuries ago, when St. James's Day approached—July 25—the pilgrimage fever would run through Europe. Hundreds and thousands of pilgrims would set off from all countries, crowding the well-trodden pilgrim road through France and across the Pyrenees. The journey to Santiago de Compostella was so popular that a pilgrimage to the shrine ranked equally with one to Rome or Jerusalem.

In 1419 there existed in Paris a special hospice for "the fraternity of St. James," which housed sixty pilgrims every day and sent them on with a small gift of money.

For several centuries the pilgrimage to St. James of Santiago was the most precious event in the lives of thousands of Englishmen and Englishwomen. Apart from the great sanctity in which the shrine was held all over Europe, it was also possible to reach it from England by sea, thus avoiding the long and dangerous journey across France and over the mountain passes into Spain.

The English voyagers, however, might well have fared better by land, for they were herded by the hundred in pilgrim ships, much as the Russians used to go to Jerusalem, and as the Moslems still go to Mecca, and if the weather in the Bay of Biscay were bad, their tortures must have been an admirable training for Purgatory.

Chaucer's Wife of Bath, who had made an extensive tour of the holy shrines, had not only visited the miraculous Virgin at Boulogne, but, as every reader of *The Canterbury Tales* will remember, she had also been "in Galice at Seint Jame."

Licences are in existence which authorize ship-owners and captains to transport pilgrims to Compostella. They cover pages in Rymer's *Foedera*. They are all in Latin, and in more or less the same terms. Here is one of them, dated 1394:

> The King, to all and each of his Admirals, greeting. Know you that we have given license to Oto Chambernoun, William Gilbert and Richard Gilbert, to receive and embark in the harbour of Dartmouth, a hundred pilgrims in a certain ship belonging to the same Oto William and Richard, called *La Charité de Paynton*, of which Peter Cork is captain: and to take them to Saint James, there to fulfil their vows, and from thence to bring them back to England, freely and without hindrance, notwithstanding any ordinances to the contrary.

Before the pilgrims were allowed to sail, they had to swear an oath not to reveal the secrets of the kingdom, or to take out of the country more money than was necessary for their journey.

Those who were left behind thought longingly of their more fortunate pilgrim friends and relations. In all the churches throughout the land little decorative altars representing the shrine of St. James—rather like the tableaux of the Nativity which appear in Catholic churches at Christmas—were built up.

Such shrines, or grottoes, were repeated on the highways, and in the streets of cities and towns, so that the devout, even if unable to kneel at the tomb at Compostella, could say their prayers before a replica of it in their own church or town.

And that is why little children in Protestant England to-day perpetuate once a year, without knowing it, a memory of the greatest shrine in Western Europe.

St. James, whose bones are still believed to lie under the gloomy cathedral of Santiago, in Galicia, was the Galilean fisherman, the brother of John and son of Zebedee. The Spanish legend is that the saint visited Spain some years after the Crucifixion, preached the Gospel, and returned to Judaea, where he was put to death by Herod Agrippa. His body was then sent by ship from Jaffa and transported under angelic guidance to the shores of Spain.

During the barbarian invasions which followed the fall of the Roman Empire, Spain returned to paganism, and the burial place of St. James was lost. It was revealed in A.D. 800 to a Galician shepherd. Other legends attribute the discovery to Thedomir, the Bishop of Ira Flavia.

It is said that a star guided the discoverer to a wood which occupied the place where Santiago now stands, and on this site of Compostella (*campus stellae*) a great church was erected in A.D. 829. It was rebuilt in a more magnificent style in A.D. 1110, and, despite exterior alterations, this is the church which still exists to-day.

Although Catholic scholars have pointed out the impos-

sibilities of the legend, the story captured the imagination
of the Middle Ages. The pilgrims put on their sandals, took
their staffs in hand and set off, to return in time wearing
in their hats the cockle shell of St. James. Shakespeare put
the following song into the mouth of Ophelia:

> *How should I my true love know*
> *From another one?*
> *By his cockle hat and staff*
> *And his sandal shoon.*

The cockle shells sewn in the pilgrim's hat were picked
up on the shores round Vigo Bay, and were the sign by
which all the Christian world recognized the person who
claimed to have visited the shrine of St. James at Santiago
de Compostella. It is many a long year since a pilgrim
wearing a cockle shell has been seen in England, but in
modern Spain such mediæval figures are occasionally encountered, as Havelock Ellis testifies in his *Soul of Spain*.
When he was in Zamora, the old town on the Duero, he
says that he found himself walking behind a dark, quiet
man, evidently just arrived from Compostella, who had
several large scallop-shells fastened to the back of his cloak,
and two or three little twisted shells hanging from the top
of the traditional palmer's staff. The author comments that
he was "an ancient figure one supposed had passed from
the earth five centuries ago, walking through the streets

of a modern city, and not even attracting the attention of the bold and familiar children of Zamora."

I think that among the many interesting features of the Cockney grottoes, and I have never heard of them in any place but London, is that occasionally the children collect contributions in an oyster shell. And oyster shells, as I have already mentioned, are nearly always a great feature of the grotto itself.

There can be no doubt that here in modern London, four centuries after the Reformation, we have a definite though unconscious memory of the scallop shell of St. James of Compostella. No doubt we can also discern in the words,

Father's gone to sea and mother's gone to fetch him back,
So please remember me.

a clear memory of pilgrims who had crossed the seas to do homage at the shrine in Spain, perhaps leaving little Londoners behind to exist on the generosity of the passer-by.

CHAPTER
22

LAMBETH DOLE

Between ten and eleven o'clock every Thursday morning twenty-nine old women knock at the gate-house of Lambeth Palace. The wicket gate is opened to reveal the cheerful features of ex-Quartermaster-Sergeant Woodward, who served through the Gallipoli campaign, although over military age at the time. For the last sixteen years he has been gatekeeper at Lambeth.

The old women enter the noble gate-house of red brick that was built by Cardinal Morton in 1490, and there they see a long wooden settle, a writing-desk, an account book, and a pen and ink.

As each woman signs the book, Mr. Woodward brings from his pocket a metal cylinder that once contained a stick of shaving soap. It is full to the lid with half-crowns. To each of the twenty-nine old women he hands one half-crown.

This is among the last relics in this country of the lavish personal charity of the Middle Ages. The weekly gift is known as Lambeth Dole. It has been in existence for six hundred years, and the money comes from the private purse of the Archbishop of Canterbury.

A few steps from the gate-house is the splendid Library of Lambeth Palace, housed in the hall that was once the dining-hall of the archbishops. In this place I sought out the history of one of the most interesting and ancient of English charities, and one that is little known even to students of London.

I unearthed a fascinating story. In 1295 Robert de Winchelsea was Archbishop of Canterbury. He was an austere and holy man. In spite of the great state in which he lived, he preserved an almost ostentatious simplicity. He gave most of his rich garments to the poor, reserving only two robes for himself. He not only helped poor scholars and beggars, but he also understood the far more difficult task of helping those who were too proud to beg. He would seek out such people and help them quietly. Much to the disgust of his servants, he was often in the habit of ordering the whole of a costly banquet to be taken away and distributed to the beggars at the gate.

It was said of Robert de Winchelsea that on Sundays and Fridays he fed four thousand poor people when corn was cheap, and five thousand when it was dear.

In this generosity he was following in the steps of prelates like Thomas à Becket who, in the preceding century, fed every day one hundred poor men and refused to sit down to eat until twenty-six beggars had been given the best dishes from his table. St. Richard of Chichester was another holy man who attempted to reconcile the temporal surroundings of a bishop with the spiritual convictions of an anchorite. He entertained sumptuously when obliged to do so, but himself sat disconcertingly at the feast, eating little or nothing. What must have been trying to his hungry, but less spiritual, guests was his habit of apostrophizing any meat or bird dish with the words, "Poor innocents, what have ye done worthy of death?" No host could develop a habit better calculated to chill the festive board. Such a man was obviously a great trial to his treasurer, and could be restrained only with difficulty from giving away the clothes on his back.

LAMBETH DOLE

The history of English charity is a subject full of interest. In early times the Church and private benevolence were responsible for feeding the thousands of hungry mouths.

Every rich man's house had a crowd of beggars at its gate, every monastery and church had a similar crowd. The poor accepted gifts as an established right and, if they begged, did so with the proud air which may still be detected in Spain, almost as if conscious that their begging confers on the donor the Christian virtue of charity.

The almost reckless lavishness of early times makes one wonder how anybody ever went hungry. It was a rule in nearly all large houses that no broken bread and meat were to be removed from the table, but were to be placed in an alms-dish and distributed to the poor.

As late as the reign of Charles II, it was a royal ordinance that no one should remove any food left on the palace tables, and that gentlemen ushers should take particular care that all food "be taken off the table upon trencher plates to be put in a basket for the poore and not indecently eaten by any servant in the room."

The Lambeth Dole is, therefore, the last relic of the ancient custom of giving away surplus food every day, or on holy days, to the local poor.

In ancient times this gift was probably a haphazard distribution of a variable quantity of broken meats, and then, as the poor gathered regularly, the gift became a daily occurrence and its quantity defined.

In 1780 the Lambeth Dole consisted of fifteen quartern loaves, nine stone of beef, and 5s. worth of half-pence. This was divided every Sunday, Tuesday, and Thursday among thirty poor parishioners at Lambeth. The beef was made into broth thickened with oatmeal, and distributed with half a loaf and twopence.

When the custom of feasting was abandoned by Archbishop Howley, in 1842, and the dining-hall of the Palace was turned into a library, the Dole was exchanged into a money payment. The sum of £200 was set aside from the Archbishop's private account to be given in weekly pensions for the loss of the broken meat. In the mid-nineteenth century the gift was 2s. to each one of thirty poor people, but in 1920 this was altered to 2s. 6d. for each of twenty-nine poor women.

The women, as if conscious that they should pay respect to one of the oldest acts of kindness in existence, put on their best clothes when they go to Lambeth Palace. They sign their names in the book and, with a word or two to cheerful Mr. Woodward, depart, carefully placing their episcopal half-crowns in little black purses. The recipients of the Lambeth Dole are chosen by the parish clergy from among hard cases of poverty. Once a recipient becomes eligible, the gift is life-long.

When the twenty-ninth old woman has departed, Mr.

Woodward closes his book and moves away from the wicket gate, as his predecessors have done every week since the reign of Edward III.

CHAPTER

23

SHEPHERD MARKET

Shepherd Market (to which many people add an inaccurate s) is one of the most satisfactory ghosts of a London that existed a hundred and fifty years ago. It is satisfactory, I think, because it is still vigorously fulfilling the functions which created it: the selling of potatoes and cabbages, beef and mutton, leather-work and china teacups; and all the rest of it.

SHEPHERD MARKET

It is a pity that so many other fragments of an older London have departed from their original intentions. They have fallen prey either to lawyers or business offices, or have otherwise been converted to uses never contemplated by their makers. But Shepherd Market owes its human interest and its vitality to an unbroken succession of small shopkeepers, who carry on, within a few yards of one of the world's most expensive thoroughfares, as if they were in Ipswich or Faversham. You might, indeed, remove the whole of Shepherd Market as it stands, with its fishmongers, butchers, fruiterers, to any old country town in England; and no one would guess that it was the very heart and core of Mayfair.

The disreputable fair in May, which gave its name to this part of London, was a fair that in mediæval times used to take place once a year round the gates of what eventually became St. James's Palace. This palace began life, perhaps in Norman times, as a hospital for female lepers. It was a good way out of London, among fields, and was dedicated, not to St. Giles, the patron saint of lepers, but to St. James-the-less. The annual Fair of St. James was granted for the upkeep of the institution by Edward I, in 1290, and, with the tenacity of a fair, it continued to be held in St. James's long after Henry VIII, having pensioned the last three leprous maidens, had turned the lazar house into a royal residence.

It was not indeed until the reign of Charles II that the

⁅ 151 ⁆

fair of St. James showed signs of migration. On the eve of
the Great Plague in 1665, it moved to a turning off the
Haymarket, but from that crowded and inconvenient site
it went westward, in 1688, to a piece of waste land on the
north side of Piccadilly, called Brookfield, because the
waters of the Tyburn ran across it. At that period the
West End of London was just rising out of the fields. Old
Bond Street, Dover Street and Berkeley Street were newly
built and looked out upon meadows. Berkeley House,
afterwards Devonshire House, faced that stretch of Piccadilly known then as Portugal Street. The architects
were exploring the site of Albemarle Street, and at that
time the silk stockings of Evelyn, the diarist, might have
been seen in the long grass, as their owner contemplated
the plans of a noble square to be called Berkeley.

So May Fair had been pushed, as fairs are generally
pushed, to the very frontier of the town. It was not a nice
fair. It attracted all the roughs and toughs of London,
who soon made the place a public scandal. Queen Anne
launched a purity campaign, but the fair had too much
vitality for her: it continued in its evil ways.

An anonymous visitor to the Fair in 1710 wrote his impressions in a rare little tract, now in the Westminster
Library, and originally in the Gardner Collection of Prints
which was sold in 1924. He describes the hideous noise of
the Fair, the theatres, the side-shows, the drinking-dens,
"where soldiers and their trulls were skipping and dancing

about to most lamentable musick," while in another part "a parcel of Scotch peddlars and their Moggies" danced "a Highlander's jig to a hornpipe."

We now began to look about us [he writes] but could not, amongst the many thousands, find one man that looked above the degree of a Gentleman's Valet, nor one whore that could have the Impudence to ask above sixpence for an hour of her cursed company. In all the Multitudes that ever I beheld, I never in my life saw such a number of Lazy, Lousy-looking Rascals and so hateful a throng of beggarly, sluttish strumpets.

Still, despite the onslaught of the moralists, I am bound to say, in justice to May Fair, that some parts of it must have been innocent enough, as the following playbill from the time of Queen Anne would seem to indicate:

This is to give notice to all Gentlemen, Ladies, and others, that, coming into May Fair, the first Booth on the left hand, over against Mr. Pinkethman's Booth, during the time of the Fair is to be seen a great collection of

STRANGE and WONDERFUL RARITIES, all alive,

FROM SEVERAL PARTS OF THE WORLD.

A little black man, lately brought from the West Indies, being the wonder of the age, he being but three foot high and twenty-five years old.

Likewise, TWO WOOD MONSTERS from the EAST INDIES, male and female, being the Admirablest Creatures that ever was seen in the Kingdom: they differ from all Creatures whatsoever; and are so wonderful in Nature that it is too large to insert here.

Also a little Marmoset from the EAST INDIES which, by a great
deal of pains, is now brought to that perfection that no creature
of his kind ever performed the like: he exercises by the word of
command; he dances the Cheshire-rounds; he also dances with
two naked swords and performs several other pretty fancies. Likewise a noble CIVET CAT from GUINY, which is admired for his
beauty and that incomparable scent which perfumes the whole
place.

VIVAT REGINA

Nothing is more difficult to kill than a fair or a street
market or a right of way. Although May Fair was banned,
it continued to be held, with its usual drums and trumpets,
tightrope walkers, conjurors, peepshows, boxers, fire-eaters,
bull-baiters, eel-divers, merry-go-rounds, and ginger-
bread-sellers, all revolving round cattle sales and heavy
drinking.

But as year followed year the buildings began to creep
nearer the fair ground. In 1738 a Mr. Edward Shepherd ob-
tained a grant to build a cattle market in the centre of the
fair ground, and for about thirty years the old fair was still
held, with Mr. Shepherd's Market as the rallying-point and
centre.

The butchers of Shepherd Market patronized a notorious public house, in what is now Hertford Street,
called "The Dog and Duck." There, as the name indicates,
was held the brutal sport of duck hunting with spaniels,
which fell out of fashion as the ponds were gradually

built over. Behind the old wooden public house lay a sheet of water nearly two hundred feet square, surrounded by a gravel walk which was unfortunately boarded up knee high to prevent the barbaric spectators from falling into the pond in their excitement. The fun consisted of seeing the duck dive from the dog.

Sometimes [says Joseph Strutt in *Sports and Pastimes of the People of England*], the duck is tormented in a different manner, without the assistance of the dogs; by having an owl tied upon her back and so put into the water, where she frequently dives in order to escape from the burden, and on her return for air, the miserable owl half drowned, shakes itself, and hooting frightens the duck; she, of course, dives again, and replunges the owl into the water. . . .

This "sport" gave way to the hardly less brutal one of pigeon shooting.

Another notorious building in Mayfair was St. George's Chapel, known as "May Fair Chapel," or "Curzon Chapel." It stood near Hertford Street. There a disreputable clergyman, Dr. Alexander Keith, would marry anyone at any hour of the day or night for a guinea, no questions asked. Illegal marriages were held there by the thousand. In the parish records of St. George's, Hanover Square, are particulars of about six thousand such unions.

The Chapel was a fruitful source of scandal in Mayfair, but the marriage which caused the greatest sensation was that of James, Duke of Hamilton and Elizabeth Gunning on February 14, 1752. The bride was the younger of the two beautiful Irish girls, nieces of the Earl of Mayo, "those goddesses, the Gunnings!" as Mary Montagu styles them in one of her letters, who set London aflame about 1750. The Duke of Hamilton fell in love with Miss Gunning at a Chesterfield House party, and became so impatient that he married her with the ring of a bed-curtain at half-past twelve at night in May Fair Chapel. Illegal marriages in May Fair, at the Fleet Prison and the Savoy Chapel became such a scandal that the Marriage Act stopped them in 1745, from which date begins the popularity of Gretna Green.

Meanwhile, the Fair, in spite of the threatening attitude of authority, continued to flourish until about 1750. A Mr. Carter, who remembered it when he was a boy, wrote an account in *The Gentleman's Magazine* of 1774. It must have been just the same old riot.

Shepherd's Market House was a building of two stories, the lower let at fair time to the gingerbread sellers and the upper to the stage players. A popular side-show at this period was the execution of puppets. This dated from the execution of Lord Lovat after the Scottish rebellion of 1745. Just as May Fair began with a reigning beauty, a rope dancer called "Lady Mary," so it ended with the wife of a Frenchman, who was to be seen in a room on the west side of Sun Court.

"The woman was short," says Mr. Carter, "but most

beautifully and delicately formed and of a lovely countenance."

She first let down her light auburn hair, which touched her knees, then, twisting it round a blacksmith's anvil, she lifted the ponderous weight from the ground.

After this a bed was laid in the middle of the room when, reclining on her back, and uncovering her bosom, the husband ordered the smiths to place thereon the anvil, and forge upon it a horseshoe! This they obeyed; by taking from the fire a red-hot piece of iron, and with their forging hammers completing the shoe, with the same might and indifference as when in the shop at their constant labour. The prostrate fair one appeared to endure this with the utmost composure, talking and singing during the whole process: then, with an effort which to the bystanders seemed like some supernatural trial, cast the anvil from off her body, jumping up at the same moment with extreme gaiety, and without the least discomposure of her dress or person. . . . She next put her foot upon a red-hot salamander. . . . Here this gratification to the senses concluded.

And so did May Fair. The low carnival that had begun in the open fields was now hemmed in by stately houses. Residents objected. Their champion was George, sixth Earl of Coventry, over whose garden wall was carried the uproar of the revelry. His lordship rose in a fury and, in the reign of George III, exerted the utmost influence at the command of an earl, which in those days was considerable, and dealt the death blow to May Fair.

Mr. Shepherd's Market remains, holding on with something of the grim tenacity of the Fair. It is still a market; it is still the heart of Mayfair. The wanderer, leaving the cosmopolitan palaces of Piccadilly, turns down White Horse Street and finds himself in what appears at first sight to be provincial England. But it is not quite that: it is the London of Dickens, which has its roots in Georgian London which, in its turn, springs from the London of the Stuarts.

The narrow alleys and the little shops have charmed many who, without inquiring into the history of Shepherd Market, are content to find themselves in what seems to have been a quieter, more peaceful age. If you go there, you cannot fail to notice the butchers' shops, and you may wonder, as I have often done, whether the inhabitants of Piccadilly and Curzon Street are abnormally carnivorous, or whether the butchers of Shepherd Market are a survival of old May Fair, which for three days every year was a live cattle and leather fair. And there is, or there was the last time I was in Shepherd Market, a leather shop whose suitcases overflow on the pavement, also, maybe, a relic of those distant days. As early as 1696 leather was one of the chief commodities of the Fair and an ancient notice, not remarkable for its grammar, states that "those that bring in leather has their ground this year gratis."

Whether such shops are the ghosts of those that existed

SHEPHERD MARKET, PICCADILLY

in Mayfair centuries ago, I cannot say. The whole of Shepherd Market is a ghost and, as London alters its appearance elsewhere, I think the Market becomes more eerie year by year.

CHAPTER

24

BIG BEN'S CRADLE

Now and then people who write to newspapers debate the question of the oldest firm in the country. I do not know if the Whitechapel Bell Foundry enters into these debates. I imagine that it does not. But this firm is, I think, the oldest firm in Great Britain—possibly in Europe—for it possesses a continuous history since the year 1570.

It was founded in the twelfth year of Elizabeth's reign

by a man named Robert Mot. In the second year of the firm's history—1572—the bells of Barnes Parish Church were cast; and they still ring every Sunday.

Eighteen years after the firm's establishment, Admiralty officials, arriving in Whitechapel in great haste, ordered Mot to stop casting church bells and to make ship's cannon instead. The guns cast in his foundry were rushed to the coast, and were used to attack the Spanish Armada.

In the course of three hundred and sixty-four years the firm has witnessed one great change: it has moved from one side of the Whitechapel Road to the other. In 1700 the ground which it now occupies was the site of an old tavern known as the "Artichoke."

As you walk along the Whitechapel Road, it is impossible to miss Mears & Stainbanks, as the Whitechapel Bell Foundry is called. Its reticence marks it out for notice in an age of ostentation. You see a queer old shop front like those which Cruikshank drew for the novels of Dickens. When you push open the door and enter, you seem to have crossed, not a doorstep, but a century. If the ghosts of the clerks who used to sit on high stools, and make laborious entries in ledgers with quill pens, could return to London, this little room is one of the few that they would recognize as an office. The old place, with its cupboards stacked with ledgers, the room upstairs with its hundreds of tuning-forks, and the little paved yard that divides the office from the foundry, have not felt the hand of Time.

When you go into the gloom of the foundry, a rambling
place with an earthen floor littered with the intractable
accessories of bell-foundries, the first thing that catches
your eye is a crane that was lifting bell metal in the reign
of Elizabeth, and is still lifting bell metal to-day. This
extraordinary relic is made of oak trees. Although the
wood has worn, it has not decayed. It looks more like
petrified stone than wood. Yet this crane lifted the bells
that were cast for the new Wren churches after the Fire
of London, and when I saw it recently its arm had just
swung round bearing a new bell for a church somewhere
in Buckingham.

As I watched the men tap a furnace and withdraw the
molten metal, and saw how the livid stream poured into
the casting, I thought that nothing has changed much in
this place for over three and a half centuries.

The Elizabethans, who made bells for a London that was
still half-timbered, and those who strove among the sparks
of the liquid metal to forge cannon for Francis Drake,
must have looked very much the same as the men—literally
their descendants—who work to-day in Whitechapel. The
technique of bell-foundry work has not altered since the
Middle Ages. There are, it is true, overhead cranes to carry
the metal. There are mechanical lathes to trim the maiden
bell.

It is no longer necessary to rebuild up a replica of the
bell before the moulds can be completed. The modern bell

is cast between two moulds, an inner and an outer mould, but the shape of the bell is still moulded in a loam made of London clay and horsehair.

Bells made in this Whitechapel foundry are pealing all over the world. Most of London's famous bells were made there. The bells of St. Clement's came from this foundry, so did the old Bow Bells, so did the bells of Westminster Abbey, the clock bells of St. Paul's and Big Ben.

Those people who still think that Big Ben is a clock are not popular at Mears & Stainbank. It is, of course, the immense bell that chimes the hours from the clock tower of the House of Commons, and although it was cast seventy-seven years ago various relics of its birth are to be discovered stacked away in the shadows of its nursery.

Hanging in a corner is a strange wooden object, rather like the rudder of a ship in shape, and about seven feet in height. There is a notice above it headed: "Big Ben's Strickle. This is the strickle that was used in the moulding of Big Ben, cast at this foundry in the year 1857."

A strickle is an instrument used in casting, and this one gives, to the technical eye, the exact dimensions, inner and outer, of Big Ben.

Big Ben has a history that perhaps few people know. In the first place he is not the original Big Ben; he is the first Big Ben melted down and recast. He takes his name, by the way, from Sir Benjamin Hall, who was First Commissioner for Works at the time.

The first Big Ben was cast in Yorkshire and was sent down to London by water. He had a frightful voyage and nearly wrecked the boat. When he was unpacked in Palace Yard, he was tested and discovered to be defective. The only thing to do was to make a new bell. Big Ben the First was accordingly sent to the Whitechapel Foundry, where he was broken up and re-melted in three furnaces fired by wood fuel. For the first time in English bell-casting, hot air was blown into the moulds all day before the metal was poured in, a method now commonly employed in the casting of all big bells.

"I'll tell you a secret about Big Ben," said a foundry-man. "He's cracked. He contains four per cent. more tin than we would have used in this foundry if we had made the metal ourselves. The weight of the first hammer used on him cracked the metal, and he's been cracked ever since. That is why Big Ben's note is different from that of any other bell. You can recognize him anywhere. That deep, and, to a bell-foundryman's ears, cracked sound, is known all over the world. The wireless has given Big Ben's defect an international reputation and it would be a pity to put him right. . . ."

After we had seen the metal cooling in the latest bell moulds, Mr. Hughes, who now owns the foundry, said:

"We'll have some lunch."

I expected him to lead the way to his favourite hotel or restaurant, but he opened a door from the counting-house and—we were in his dining-room, where a leg of lamb was ready on the table.

What memories of the old times this place awakens, one of the last factories whose owner calls his men by their Christian names, one of the last places where the owner lives, works, eats and sleeps on the premises.

CHAPTER

25

ℓEECH ℳERCHANT

Once a week an aeroplane from Le Bourget carries to London a cargo that would horrify the passengers, were they aware of it. Five hundred hungry leeches are mailed to a firm of chemists who began business in Fleet Street a hundred and twenty years ago as "leech merchants."

This shop, under the arch of Holborn Viaduct, is one of the few places in London to-day where you can buy *hirudo medicinalis,* which is the technical term for the unpleasant little water-worm that has been used since remote times for blood-letting.

Many people think that leeches went out of fashion at least a century ago; in fact, certain well-known encyclopædias might lead one to believe that the trade in them has entirely ceased. But this is not so. There is a regular demand in London every week for five hundred leeches. They go to hospitals and to doctors. Some chemists' shops in the Wimpole Street district always keep a supply of them in glass jars.

The word "leech" comes from an Anglo-Saxon word, *laece,* which means "one who heals." Medical books in Saxon days were called "leech-books," and the term "leech," often used contemptuously for a doctor, survived until recent times.

It is wrong, however, to believe, as many do, that this nickname was given because doctors in the age of wholesale blood-letting were over-fond of leeches. It is the other way about. The leech received its name untold centuries ago from the doctor.

I went into the shop in Farringdon Street one morning and asked to see some leeches. A man stood behind the counter in a white jacket and apron.

"In the chilly weather," he said, "we keep them near the stove."

He went to an inner room and returned with a round tin as large as a wash-basin. The top was carefully stopped with a cover made of several thicknesses of sacking:

"If there's a hole as small as a pin head," explained the man, "they'll get through."

He carefully untied the string and removed the sacking. In a few inches of water, and crawling with deliberate precision round the inside of the tin, and adhering to the underside of the sacking lid, was the latest consignment of five hundred leeches. They had crossed the Channel that morning. The creatures are caught in the Gironde, in the south-west of France. I believe the art of "leech fishing" is an ancient and unpleasant employment. The "fisherman" walks bare-legged into the marsh and knows at once when he has had a bite. He detaches the leech from his leg, places it in a tin, and goes on.

"These leeches," said the man, "are the speckled variety. Have a look."

He plunged his hand into the water and held a fistful of leeches towards me. He playfully dropped them back into the water and picked up another handful. As he talked, he kept moving his fingers and caressing the creatures; this was to keep them on the move. Nevertheless, one of them fixed itself firmly between his fingers, and he had to pull hard to get it off.

"That one nearly drew blood," he said.

"They're beautifully marked," said the chemist. "I won't

ask you to hold one, because I can see you won't, but let me take them over to the light."

They were slightly flattened greenish-black creatures about two and a half inches long. They were mottled on the under side and had several rows of reddish and yellowish spots along the back. They were never still.

"I've been handling leeches for fifty years," said the chemist, in reply to my remark that he is probably the only man in London who would care to place his hand in such a tin.

"In the old days we used to get two thousand leeches a week from a doctor at Notting Hill. I don't know where he got them from. The ordinary English leech isn't suitable for medical use, although I believe that centuries ago Norfolk used to supply most of the leeches used by London doctors. In the last fifty years the use of leeches has gradually fallen away. I suppose thousands of doctors would not know how to apply a leech, or how to make him bite if he didn't feel like it.

"Still, we sell five hundred a week. Bart's has a regular twenty-five at a time. They like them nice and fresh. The Ophthalmic Hospital has them too. There are some eye inflammations that can only be relieved by the application of a leech. You must always let a leech feed until he's full and then he drops off and . . ."

"Forgive me for pointing out," I interrupted, "that the big green one has got a firm grip between your fingers."

"I know," he said. "I'm letting him take hold just to show you the kind of wound they make."

After a rather stiff struggle, he pulled the leech away and showed me a small white mark between his fingers from which blood began to flow so rapidly that he had to open a packet of lint and bandage his hand.

The retail price of a leech is fourpence. It is, perhaps, surprising that a great firm of wholesale chemists should still traffic in such an apparently unremunerative trade.

It may be, however, that this leech trade is largely sentimental, because the firm was founded by Henry Potter, the descendant of generations of Buckinghamshire yeomen, who began in a modest way as a leech merchant, seedsman and herbalist, one hundred and twenty years ago.

Potter soon discovered that leech-mongering was a highly profitable trade, although he was not by any means the only leech merchant in London at that time. He lived at a house called Streatham Place, at the top of Brixton Hill, at that time a country district.

In front of his house was a round pond, in which he kept his stock. As he progressed in business, he opened other aquaria and always had many thousands of leeches ready for sale. In 1845, the year before Henry Potter retired from business, the London hospitals were using 50,000 leeches every year.

At that time the best leeches came from Smyrna. It was the difficulty of receiving supplies at regular intervals that led to such leech ponds and breeding-places as those established by Potter.

The shop in Farringdon Street is therefore an interesting link with a trade that has been in existence for centuries. One may imagine that, when Farringdon Street is hushed at night, the ghost of a Georgian physician comes tapping along with his gold-headed cane, to pause before the door of the only place in London where he could obtain his ancient and blood-thirsty ally.

LAST OF THE
HUGUENOT WEAVERS

In a neat little house in a dreary street on the boundary of Spitalfields an old man and his sister work all day at two hand looms. Those complicated structures, which even science has not been able to simplify, occupy the entire bedroom space in the house and, as you go in, you must press yourself into a narrow space between the looms. The weavers start work at 8 o'clock and stop at 8 in the evening. When darkness falls, they light an oil lamp and continue to weave lengths of costly silk.

The name of this old man and his sister is Poyton, which still carries a French sound with it, and they will tell you that two hundred and fifty years ago their ancestor was smuggled out of France and across the Channel in a sugar-crate. The Poytons are among the last descendants of the Huguenots to weave silk by hand in Spitalfields. There are not more than sixteen or eighteen of these old weavers left, and when they die the last link between the Huguenots and hand-loom weaving in London will be broken for ever.

There must be many people in this country who do not know that several centuries ago their ancestors were French. The Huguenot refugees quickly identified themselves with this country and in a few generations merged their nationality, until to-day there is often nothing but a surname such as Leroy, Meux, Dubois, Merceron, Chabot—or English variants of such names—to point to their French origin.

On the other hand, many people of Huguenot descent are proud of that fact and belong to the Huguenot Society of London. This society was founded in 1885 for the study of Huguenot history and to bind together men and women of Huguenot ancestry.

Early Huguenot settlers, who might be termed French Puritans, came over to London long before the horrible massacre of St. Bartholomew's Eve in 1550. Edward VI gave them the use of the Dutch Church of Austin Friars.

Twenty-two years later, on the eve of St. Bartholomew's
Day, a bell tolled in Paris at the hour of midnight. It was
the signal for doors to be beaten down and for Protestants
to be slaughtered in their beds. It has been said that seventy
thousand Huguenots were murdered that night in Paris and
in the provinces. The few who were able to escape came to
England to spread the tale of their sorrow.

The great settlement came later, however, when persecu-
tion started afresh after the revocation of the Edict of
Nantes in 1685. The ports and the roads of France were
watched for escaping Huguenots. Thousands were im-
prisoned and sent as slaves to the galleys. In spite of the
vigilance, however, eighty thousand Huguenots came to
England between 1686 and 1688, and fifteen thousand of
them settled in Spitalfields, Long Acre, Soho and Seven
Dials. Among them were some of the finest silk-weavers
in France. Their arrival in this country meant an entirely
new day for the silk industry. Thanks to them, Spitalfields
soon became the flourishing centre of English silk-weaving.

Years before the great Huguenot invasion James I had
interested himself in silk and had attempted to grow English
silk-worms in a series of "Mulberry Gardens," one of which
was planted on the ground afterwards occupied by Buckingham Palace. With the arrival of the skilled French
weavers, the industry began to prosper. In one year—1719
—over £300,000 worth of silk hoods and scarves for women
were made in London. In Queen Anne's reign about fifty

HUGUENOT WEAVERS

thousand people were engaged in the Spitalfields silk-weaving, most of them English weavers working under the direction of the Huguenots. They introduced the weaving of lustrings, alamodes, brocades, satins, paduasoys, damasks, taffetas and black velvets.

The work that Mr. Poyton, his sister, and a few other old people do, is piece-work for the silk factory of Vavasseur & Co. I watched Miss Poyton weaving a square of silk for Old Etonian ties. From these two I heard the story that I have heard so often from the lips of hand-loom weavers in England, Wales, Scotland and Ireland.

"The young people won't come to the loom," they said. "It's too much like hard work. They won't sit at it from light until dark, as we have done all our lives. Young people to-day want jobs which make it easy for them to get off to the cinema and to the dance hall. When we go, there is no one to come after us."

If you go after dark into this street in Spitalfields, you will hear the ghostly clack-clack-clack of the Poytons' shuttles in the upper room. It is a sound that links to-day with the sound of the bell that tolled in Paris on St. Bartholomew's Eve, three hundred and sixty-three years ago.

CHAPTER

27

ALE AND EYE LOTION

A number of strange ghosts haunt the public-houses of London. There is, for instance, the "Green Man" in Edgware Road.

If you go into this place and ask, not for beer, but for eye lotion, the man behind the bar will take down a large bottle that stands amid the whisky and the gin, and he will, without question, measure out an ounce or two.

This is a custom whose origin must be sought far beyond the eighteenth century. In it we may see a vision of the ghosts of the maidens of Edgware, who were in the habit, centuries ago, of drawing water from a spring that was believed to have marvellous healing properties.

The time came, however, when buildings began to advance from the present Marble Arch along the Edgware Road, and one day the local people learnt with fear and anger that their magic spring was threatened. A tavern was to be built over it.

They objected so strenuously and so successfully, that a clause was inserted in the lease of the tavern stipulating that the landlord must give, to any customer who asked for it, a glass of the healing water from his cellar. The arrangement worked well. The inhabitants of the Edgware Road had not only their ancient spring, but also a fountain of stronger waters.

But the time came when the underground railway tunnelled almost under the "Green Man." Something happened to the ancient spring, and it had to be bricked over. But the "Green Man" continued to give away eye lotion.

"We have it made up at the chemist's," said the present proprietor, when I questioned him about the custom. "We always keep a bottle in the bar, because we never know when we shall be asked for it."

He produced a large flagon of eye lotion.

"It is no better than you can get from any chemist," he

said. "The old spring is a thing of the past. I suppose we keep up the custom because the grandfathers of people who come to the 'Green Man' were in the habit of getting this lotion from us, and their grandchildren sometimes ask for it. Oh, yes, we have two or three requests every week."

Then there is the "Castle Inn," in Cowcross Street, not far from Farringdon Street railway station. If you go into this place, unstrap your wrist-watch and ask the proprietor how much he will advance on it, a gleam of unhappy understanding will flit across his features.

Beneath the clock in the old-fashioned mahogany bar hang the three gold balls of the Medici and a framed copy of the Pawnbroking Act. The "Castle Inn" is, in spite of itself, technically a pawnbroker's shop.

They will tell you that it is nine years since anyone seriously tried to pawn anything there, and consequently their sense of pawning has become atrophied.

"We shouldn't know how to do it," they say.

The ghost behind this strange custom is the substantial one of a large and florid man who came in during the middle of the eighteenth century and tried to raise money on a ring or trinket. The man was George IV.

In those days Hockley at the Hole, Old Clerkenwell, was a great place for cock-fighting. Presumably the monarch had been to a fight with some of his gay friends, and, having lost every penny, was in desperate need of ready money.

In recognition of the landlord's kindness in raising money for him, the "Castle Inn" was created a pawnshop by charter, long before the Pawnbroking Act of 1872 became law.

Another strange custom is still carried out in the "Widow's Son," near Bromley-by-Bow Station. In this public-house a large bundle of dry currant buns hangs from the ceiling.

The story goes that somewhere about the year 1823 a widow, whose only son was drowned at sea, used to set the table every Good Friday and wait for his return. Every year she would place a hot-cross-bun ready for him. Her cottage became known as the Bun House.

When she died, the cottage was pulled down and the "Widow's Son" tavern was erected in its place. I have read that the custom of adding a bun to the ancient collection that hangs from the roof is provided for by clause in the lease, but I do not know from personal investigation if this is so or not.

Much the same kind of story is that behind "Dirty Dick's," in Bishopsgate, whose underground bar, although covered with cherished cobwebs and decorated with the skeletons of rats and cats, manages to look pleasantly clean.

"Dirty Dick's" wine vaults commemorate one of the most notorious personages of London a hundred and twenty years ago, a man called Nicholas Bentley, whose effect on his contemporaries was such that the *Dictionary of National Bi-*

ography devotes a column to him.

Bentley, the son of a wealthy merchant of Leadenhall Street, was, in his youth, a man of airs and graces. It is recorded that he visited France to attend the coronation of Louis XVI, was presented to the king, and was generally considered "the handsomest and best-dressed English gentleman then at the French Court." In London he was known as "the beau of Leadenhall Street."

He began, however, to develop eccentricities. He would be seen one day in the height of fashion, wearing powdered hair and a rich blue coat, and the next he would appear covered with dirt, his hair all over his face. As he grew older, the second mood took complete possession of him, and he seems himself to have chosen the name of "Dirty Dick," by which the whole of London began to know him.

He locked himself in his warehouse at 46, Leadenhall Street, and allowed the dust and filth of years to accumulate round him. All kinds of stories were whispered. It was said that he slept in his own coffin, and that he had a secret Bluebeard's room in his mildewed mansion in which the bodies of women were concealed.

A less gruesome story was that the house contained a room set ready for his wedding breakfast, but, when the news was brought on his wedding morning that his bride had died, the place was shut up, the windows barred, the door fastened, and he resolved never to enter it, or permit any one else to do so, as long as he lived. William Granger, who gives many details of "Dirty Dick" in his *Wonderful Museum,* comments that "this story is by several supposed to be merely a fabrication to satisfy the curious."

Granger prints an eye-witness account of the premises in Leadenhall Street after "Dirty Dick" was forced to leave them, the lease having terminated. The house became one of the sights of London, and two thousand persons visited it during the first fortnight that it was thrown open to the curious.

An engraving was published at the time, showing visitors prodding about in the accumulated dirt of thirty years, women drawing their skirts away from the dust and the filth as they gazed at the overhanging cobwebs and the knee-deep litter on the floor.

Bentley was forced to leave his dirty warehouse in February, 1804. He removed to Jewry Street, Aldgate, where he lived for three years, and then to Leonard Street, Shoreditch, where, after twelve months, he adopted a roving life, wandering about the country like a tramp.

The poor old man died in Scotland, and is, I believe, buried in the lovely old Abbey Church beside the river at Haddington, where Jane Welsh Carlyle lies beneath the touching epitaph of her difficult Sage of Chelsea.

"Dirty Dick's" in Bishopsgate is, therefore, a ghost of that strange house in Leadenhall Street which piqued the curiosity of our ancestors at the beginning of the last century; and right nobly has it lived up to its reputation.

CHAPTER
28

THE "LION SERMON"

There is a macabre humour about many of our London ghosts. I refer to those gifts of money left in ancient times on the understanding that certain conditions in a will are faithfully observed year after year.

I think any solicitor will bear me out when I say that there is a limit to the things one may ask a beneficiary to perform in order to obtain the money; but the law allows a whimsical latitude. For instance, if one's desires are eccentric but harmless, such as the wish for a dance round one's grave on Midsummer Night, it is certain that, if the legacy makes it worth while, such a dance will be held.

Among the many curious duties imposed on present and future generations are periodic inspections of vaults and graves, such as that laid down in the will of Mary Gibson, of Hampstead, who died in 1773.

She left £5,000 in bank stock, the interest to be spent in keeping in order the family tomb at Sutton. She left a further sum, the interest on which was to be spent as follows: £5 to the rector of the church for a service and sermon on the anniversary of her death, £5 for the poor of Hampstead, £4 for the churchwarden, and £1 for the clerk of the church in which the sermon was preached. All these legacies were, however, dependent on the condition that the Governors of Christ's Hospital should open the vault at Sutton every year and satisfy themselves that everything was in good order. Should the Governors fail in their annual inspection, the money would pass to the Foundling Hospital. So far, the Governors of Christ's Hospital have complied with the terms of the will. Every year on August 12 they open the vault in Sutton and satisfy themselves that everything is in order.

The Mayor of St. Ives, in Cornwall, complies with similar conditions. Every five years, in company with a fiddler, ten little girls, the daughters of tinners, fishermen or seamen, and a number of old women, he climbs the hill at the back of the town, to visit the tomb of John Knill, who was customs officer at St. Ives in 1762. The old women and the little girls dance round the tomb while the fiddler plays a jig.

On the observance of this strange custom depends a whole series of charities; and up and down the country every year similar queer things happen so that living men and women may reap the benefit of legacies. Many centuries ago a popular form of imposing obligations on future generations was to leave money on condition that, on a given day, a certain type of sermon must be preached in a stipulated pulpit.

I have read in Dr. George C. Williamson's book, *Curious Survivals,* that an annual sermon against witchcraft is preached in Huntingdon parish church. I regret to say that I have never heard this.

The London City companies have naturally accumulated a number of unusual commitments in the course of their long existence. On a stated day the master and members of a company may assemble and listen solemnly to a sermon ordered by a man long dead. The Stationers' Company, for instance, assemble once a year in Hendon parish church to hear a sermon preached on the text, "Human life is a bubble"; words which are just as good to-day as they were when Richard Johnson chose them in 1795.

If you are passing the old church of St. Catherine Cree,

in Leadenhall Street, on October 16, you should go inside
to listen to the "Lion Sermon." It has been preached without interruption, year after year, for two hundred and
eighty-six years, to commemorate the escape of Sir John
Gaymer from a lion.

Sir John lived in the reign of Charles I. He was a merchant adventurer who had made a fortune in the Levan-
tine trade. He was knighted by Charles I and became Lord
Mayor of London during the Commonwealth.

Gaymer seems to have landed himself in trouble with
the Parliamentarians by resisting the order for compulsory
military service, an order which was so unpopular with the
City apprentices that the Commons were forced to withdraw it after three days.

In company with four aldermen, the unfortunate Lord
Mayor was flung into prison in the Tower, from which
point of comparative safety he began to assail his enemies
in a number of admirably written pamphlets.

He remained in prison for two years, all the time crying
in print and out of print for justice and a jury. The Parliamentarians, however, appointed another Lord Mayor
of London and gave Gaymer a chance to make his peace by
kneeling as a delinquent at the Bar of the House of Commons.

But the stubborn old man did not choose to humiliate
himself. He was then fined £500 for contempt and sent
back to the Tower. His release came too late for him to

enjoy what triumph there may have been in it, for he died the same year, worn out with his fight for trial by jury.

Nothing, however, in his stormy old life can have impressed him so much as his encounter with a lion. This occurred when he was lost in a desert, during one of his trading ventures to the East. As he blundered on, hoping to strike the right path, a lion appeared and gazed attentively at him. Sir John fell on his knees and prayed that the lion would not attack him. He made vows of charity. To his delight, the creature cast on him a final glance of disapproval and bounded away.

The old merchant was true to his vow. Many institutions to-day, which have been receiving a grant of money for centuries, owe gratitude to the magnanimous king of beasts.

The "Lion Sermon," which is preached every year from the pulpit of St. Catherine Cree, is, however, Gaymer's chief work of commemoration. It has never lapsed, and has been preached since the reign of Charles I. It should not be a difficult sermon to write, full, as the story of Gaymer and the lion is, of excellent material for moralization. How true it is that many of us forget to be charitable until we have been adequately scared.

CHAPTER
29

MAUNDY MONEY

An interesting memory of Catholic England takes place
in Westminster Abbey on Thursday in Holy Week. It is
known as the Royal Maundy.

It is widely believed that the word Maundy comes from
the maunds, or baskets, used during this ceremony to
hold the gifts for the poor, but as the word was employed
long before baskets had anything to do with the ceremony,

the connexion is obviously inaccurate.

Professor Skeat seems to have solved the mystery of this word by tracing it to the French *mande*, or the Latin *mandatum*, which was the first word of the anthem sung during the service.

The Kings of England have from time immemorial given gifts to the poor and entertained poor men and women on Maundy Thursday. Nowadays Their Majesties go to Westminster Abbey to watch the distribution of the Royal Maundy, which is a gift of money to poor men and women who correspond in number to the years of the monarch's age.

The Yeomen of the Guard attend this ceremony in full dress, and carry in a huge dish on which the leather money bags are stacked, the old-fashioned leather purse-strings hanging over the edge of the dish like a fringe. The gift, which is handed out by the Lord High Almoner, is made in two distributions:

The First distribution:

£1 15s. in lieu of clothing to each woman.
£2 5s. in lieu of clothing to each man.

The Second distribution:

A Red Purse containing £1 in gold and £1 10s., an allowance in lieu of provisions formerly given in kind.

A White Purse containing as many pence as the King is years

of age, and given in silver pennies, twopences, threepences and fourpences.

This money, which is all freshly minted for the Royal Maundy, is made with unmilled edges.

The prayer which is said just before the distribution gives the clue to the origin of the ceremony:

Lord Jesus Christ, who when about to institute the Holy Sacrament at Thy last supper, didst wash the feet of Thy Apostles, teaching us by Thy example the grace of humility: Cleanse us, we beseech Thee, from all filth of sin, that we may be worthy partakers of Thy holy Mysteries.

Although altered in form, the Royal Maundy is the ancient ceremony of Washing the Feet, which, from the fourth century onwards, was a ceremony observed by the Pope, kings, prelates and great nobles.

The King of England, in common with all other Catholic monarchs, was in the habit of girding on a towel and kneeling in turn before a number of beggars, washing their feet and afterwards providing a meal for them.

In this way the story of the Last Supper was dramatized and the King gave in public an object-lesson in the virtue of humility which may, or may not, have appeared convincing.

I think the last king to perform the Washing of the Feet was ex-King Alfonso of Spain. Before the War the rite was also carried out with much ceremony by the Emperor of Austria.

The ceremony survives in its full glory among the Greek Orthodox and the Eastern Churches in Jerusalem. I have described in my book on Palestine how, on Maundy Thursday, the Greek Patriarch and twelve bishops occupy a green wooden stage in the courtyard of the Holy Sepulchre, how the Patriarch disrobes, girds on a towel and, kneeling down before the twelve bishops, who remove their shoes or boots, carefully washes and dries their feet.

The Armenian Church observes the same ceremony, using soft butter instead of soap. I believe the child-like Abyssinians perform the act with great thoroughness and with the help of a cake of Sunlight.

Queen Elizabeth always observed the ceremony with great care; but she took equal care that the pauper's feet had been previously washed by the yeomen of the laundry in warm water and sweet herbs.

Pepys, in his diary for April 4, 1667, says that he went to Whitehall to see Charles II perform the ceremony; but it was enacted for him by the Bishop of London.

The last English monarch to wash the feet of the poor at Easter time was James II; but it was performed by a deputy as recently as 1731. In that year the Archbishop of York acted for the King.

During the last century and a half, so great have been the changes in the observation of the Royal Maundy that

YEOMEN WITH THE ROYAL MAUNDY, WESTMINSTER ABBEY

its original meaning has been almost totally obscured. The act of feet-washing, the whole purpose of the ceremony, has been discontinued, and the gifts of clothes and food have been assessed in terms of money.

There is only one clue to the original ceremony: all the officials connected with the Royal Almonry wear cloths or linen scarves during the distribution of the Maundy. These symbolize the towels once used at the washing of the feet.

The Maundy money, although minted in obsolete denominations, is current coin of the realm and should be accepted as legal tender anywhere, although I would not like to promise that it would be willingly received.

This question, however, does not arise, because the annual Maundy money is of value to collectors of coins, and the recipients of the purses can, if they care to do so, always make a profit on the ancient bounty.

CHAPTER
30

RED DRAGON'S OFFICE

Although Queen Victoria Street is dignified at one end by the offices of *The Times*, and at the other by the Bank of England, it has always seemed to me an inappropriate fate that has stranded the College of Arms there, like an old helmet washed up in a busy harbour.

The ancient custodian of the nation's legitimacy—possibly the only institution that has no doubt about the definition of the word "gentleman"—is completely out of place in a thoroughfare whose solitary martial note is sounded by the cornets of the Salvation Army.

What can the shades of Poitiers and the Field of the Cloth of Gold have in common with typewriters, broom-handles, patent medicines, newsprint and bath tubs, and all the thousand and one common-places of modern life which Queen Victoria Street, with the rest of the world, now considers more important than Norman blood?

Yet on the other hand, where in a perfect London would you place the College of Arms? Near the War Office, to lend that department something of the romance and tradition which departed during the last War? Or among the museums of South Kensington? I do not know.

Of all the ghosts of London, the thirteen officials of the College of Arms are, to my mind, among the most interesting and certainly the most spectacular. They possess the most ancient official status in the realm. I understand that there have been no serious staff changes in the College since 1480.

I have been to this building many times to consult old documents, and on each occasion I recapture the feeling of fantasy which pervaded my first arrival.

"Is Rouge Dragon in?" I managed to ask the door-keeper, fighting down, as I did so, a strong feeling of improbability.

"No, sir," he replied, "Rouge Dragon is out."

This seemed a dramatic and rather fearsome remark. It was as if, passing through the Zoo turnstile, a keeper had mentioned that one of the lions had escaped. Rouge Dragon was out!

Somewhere in London, made more terrible to the imagination, perhaps, by the thin disguise of a bowler hat and a blue overcoat, Rouge Dragon was at large, mixing with the crowds, perhaps sitting on the top of an omnibus; perhaps even calling at a shop to buy a tin of tobacco like any ordinary human being!

"Is Bluemantle in?" I asked.

"He's not here this week."

"Well, could I see Rouge Croix?"

"You'd better see Portcullis, sir. I'll run up and see if he's disengaged."

That is the way they talk in this strange, red-brick building in Queen Victoria Street, where the mighty thunder of Agincourt has faded to a thin murmur, a murmur as thin and crisp as bank-notes crackling, to whose accompaniment the heralds compose armorial bearings for knights dubbed on the fields of party.

While you stand, waiting for the doorkeeper to return and say that Portcullis can see you, it would not appear at all unusual if Mr. Burke galloped into the forecourt on a unicorn, bearing in his hands the latest edition of his *Landed Gentry*, or if Mr. Debrett, leading a leopard, temporarily uncouchant, came to deposit among the archives a fine bar sinister.

When you go inside, you stand in the great panelled hall where, only a century ago, the Earl Marshal and Garter King of Arms decided points of chivalry, and attempted to solve delicate points of honour for which there is not, and never has been, a better solution than a cold morning and a couple of rapiers.

But the fantasy of the building increases as you mount the stairs. It is the only building in London in which that lean and beloved Knight of La Mancha would, perhaps, be entirely at home.

Above every door are bright quarterings and the names of officials: "Garter King of Arms," "Norroy, King of Arms," "Clarenceux, King of Arms."

Then come the six Heralds: Lancaster, Somerset, York, Chester, Richmond, and Windsor, and the four Pursuivants: Rouge Dragon, Rouge Croix, Portcullis and Bluemantle.

There they are in modern London, with the red omnibuses thundering up Queen Victoria Street outside, the successors of the men who lifted their trumpets at Harfleur and Rouen, who turned over the slain and wrote out the casualty lists at Agincourt.

The brilliant world in which the Heralds once lived has vanished to a symbol on a finger ring, or an occasional crest upon a perambulator in Hyde Park. But every day the Pursuivants ride to the College of Arms; but, alas, they ride by Underground.

But what do they do to-day? If you open a door with "Rouge Dragon" on it, you will see, instead of the man in plate armour who, of course, ought to be there, a man in striped trousers very like any barrister in his chambers.

Heralds, who are paid on the Tudor scale of remuneration, which is about £16 a year, are always delighted to discover any members of the public who wish to stamp a coat of arms on their notepaper. It costs about £75 to take out new armorial bearings, and another £50 for a badge which female members of the family can embroider on cushions or engrave on their cigarette-cases.

When the United States were rich, the Heralds were happy searching out ancestors for wealthy Americans; but since the slump, rich Americans seem to have lost interest in their origin.

The College of Arms is also the official repository of all state ceremonial procedure. It is still the duty of the Heralds to proclaim war, and to announce the death and accession of kings.

They have also under their charge an enormous genealogical library that contains the roots of every old family in England and Wales. This library proves how, since the Wars of the Roses, the aristocracy of this country has been recruited from the common people.

Unlike certain countries, whose aristocracy has remained rigid and exclusive, that of England is the history of wave

HERALDS AT TEMPLE BAR

after wave of men putting aside the merchant's bonnet or the soldier's cap to assume a coronet. It is an interesting library. It contains the fantastic family claims of ancient times, and it contains also the beautifully documented modern work of the College of Arms, which has, during the last half century, placed genealogy and heraldry on an entirely new and reliable basis.

In spite of their modern functions, the Kings at Arms, the Heralds and the Pursuivants, are strange survivals from an age that is dead. Their pens are now mightier than their swords. Their scholarship is more important than their fanfares. But when they ride out on any great occasion, we see for a brief moment one of the links that binds the present to the past.